NIJENRODE STUDIES IN BUSINESS 4

Business is a broad field where science and business reality can and should meet to analyse and discuss old theories and to develop new ones, applicable for modern managers. One of the main objectives of the ***Nijenrode studies in business*** *is to give a push to new developments in the multidisciplinary business area, to serve the profession as well as a wider audience.*

PROJECT SET STRATEGIES

PROJECT SET STRATEGIES

FRANS G. J. DERKINDEREN
Netherlands School of Business

ROY L. CRUM
University of Florida

Martinus Nijhoff Publishing
Boston / The Hague / London

Distributors for North America:
Martinus Nijhoff Publishing
Kluwer Boston, Inc.
160 Old Derby Street
Hingham, Massachusetts 02043

Distributors outside North America:
Kluwer Academic Publishers Group
Distribution Centre
P.O. Box 322
3300 AH Dordrecht, The Netherlands

Library of Congress Cataloging in Publication Data

Derkinderen, F
Project set strategies.

(Nijenrode studies in business ; v. 4)
1. Industrial management. 2. Business. 3. Business enterprises – Finance. I. Crum, Roy L., joint author. II. Title. III. Series.
HD31.D473 658.1'5 79-15544
ISBN 0-89838-014-6

Printed in the United States of America

To Joyce and Willy

CONTENTS

LIST OF FIGURES

LIST OF TABLES

PREFACE

Project Set Strategies focuses on an issue of vital concern to corporate managers: the development and implementation of strategy. Regretfully, this topic has received too little attention in the literature of finance and has been treated incompletely in the management journals. In fact, not everyone recognizes that it falls within the sphere of finance. However, since the important issues discussed in this book strategically shape the destiny of the company and can seal its fate long before the point is reached where conventional finance considerations come into play, it is essential that this recognition be acknowledged.

From the management point of view, it has long been realized that strategic elements play a crucial role in the continued well-being of the firm. Nevertheless, this truth is overlooked to some extent with most management techniques since there is insufficient typification, often leading to unjustified generalizations and inadequate attention to the requirements of the specific situation. Also, these management techniques are not grounded upon the long-established financial economic theories of valuations and thus can lead to misdirected guidance.

Since the two academic disciplines of "management" and "finance" have much insight to offer each other, this book represents an effort to link the strategic management area to a theoretically sound and usable financial economic foundation. In this way, the probability of errors of omission or unjustified generalizations is decreased and help is offered for ascertaining more relevant goal-directed recommendations.

We owe many debts of gratitude to various people and institutions. We must first and foremost thank Nijenrode, Netherlands School of Business, for the very generous financial and other support given to the project. Without this support, the book would not have been possible. Second, the College of Business Administration of the University of Florida must be acknowledged for the resources that were made available to us. Third, the very able assistance of Joyce C. Crum in preparing, editing, and proofing many versions of the manuscript contributed substantially to the successful completion of the project.

Kees van Zuijlen in an early phase and Toine van Hoof toward the end of the research process must be acknowledged for providing valuable assistance with parts of the manuscript. Also, we are grateful for the services provided by G.B.J. Bomers, J.W. Gotcher, A.L. de Joode, E. Lucas, J.S. Mackenzie Owen, St. J.B. Nixon, J. Rassers, J.T. Severiens, and R.S. Tijmstra. Finally, we must thank our families for understanding, patience, and building up our courage to continue when problems arose. Any errors remaining are solely our responsibility.

PROJECT SET STRATEGIES

1 INTRODUCTION TO PROJECT SET PREPLANNING

It has long been recognized that prosperity, if not the survival of a firm, is more than a matter of luck. Instead of simply muddling through, it involves, among other things, experience, insight, intuition, and innovation, all coming together to focus on what the firm should be and what actions are required to achieve the objectives.

The name usually associated with this focusing process is *strategic planning. Strategic* generally implies the long term, or at least sufficiently far into the future for the impacts of currently conceived actions to work their way through the corporation. *Planning* can be seen as the setting of courses of action to move from a current to a desired position, taking into consideration the circumstances of the context within which the entity is constrained to act.

This type of planning can be conceived and formalized in terms of written rules, or it can be done informally, without explicitly formulated guidelines. Similarly it can be conducted either mainly in accordance with the wishes of a dominant manager or by consensus among several coequal managers. Independent of the form that planning assumes, however, the need to plan is increasing because of ever higher stakes; but at the same time it is becoming more and more difficult to accomplish successfully. There are two primary reasons for this: increasing environmental complexity and the necessity for explicit consideration of dynamics.

As the complexity of the environment increases, the number of feasible alternatives that confront the firm expands geometrically, hindering the ability of management to identify the "best" (or even one of the best) course of action to include in the plan. When, on top of this heightened complexity, more dynamics are added, the time span over which a firm can be expected to make reasonably accurate forecasts shortens. In many cases, it is no longer judicious to assume that long-range forecasts can be made with the required degree of accuracy for setting plans.

Confronted at the same time with an increasing need to plan and a decreasing ability to make the long-range forecasts required for successful planning, the resourceful manager must find a way to wring every salient piece of information from available data. Once obtained, this information can be used in a structured manner to position the firm as advantageously as possible to meet the challenges of the environment as they arise.

Because of these complexities and environmental dynamics, concentrating attention on those variables that can be forecasted with reasonable reliability in order to develop an applicable course of action in main lines is called for. Further, adequate attention is needed to develop timely and built-in relevant capabilities to maintain the flexibility to respond as appropriate to the as yet indistinct. This is vital for a sound approach to management. In this chapter, a methodology that can serve as an aid for accomplishing these tasks—preplanning—is described and placed in the proper perspective.

PREPLANNING THE FIRM'S PROJECT SET

The project set of a company represents the aggregation of all activities, or strategic business units (SBUs), in which the firm is either engaged or wishes to become involved.[1] For very small firms, there might be a single SBU concentrated at one geographic location. Other firms will usually be diversified into several different SBUs, into multiple geographic production and/or marketing areas, or, as is quite often the case, the spread may be in terms of both SBUs and geographic areas. The structure of the company becomes more complex when the number of different SBUs and geographic areas included under the corporate umbrella increases. As a consequence, the problems of management become more diverse and numerous. Managing a large and intricate organization takes on a singularly distinctive character that is substantially different from running a smaller firm. No longer can an individual hope to possess all of the time, knowledge, and skill required to coordinate and direct the activities of the various elements. Delegation of authority is necessary.

This delegation of authority creates problems of its own. Each submanager competes with all other submanagers for a share of the corporate resources. Effective and efficient allocation of the resources demands careful coordination of the activities and an informed weighing of the merits of each contending use. However, the most deserving use may not be represented by the current operations. Since there is no "invisible hand" to effect the most desirable allocation, management often has to cope with difficult choices.

Preparation for the right decisions under these complex circumstances is effective only if there is a prior conception of what the company wants to achieve and how its goals can be realized. This is the very essence of strategy. What is more, for adequate decision preparation, strategy must be conceived as a dynamic concept that is under a process of evolution. The business world is changing. If strategy does not adapt to the shifting environment of the firm under review, it will become dated, obsolete, and ineffectual.

A methdology designed to aid management in developing a sound allocation strategy and in monitoring the appropriateness of and adherence to this strategy is called *preplanning.* It refers to the process of determining the direction of movement of the firm's strategic posture, including appropriate actions that need to be taken to move in the intended direction, supplemented, if possible, by a rough but situationally conditioned indication of the magnitude and rate of change of this movement as far as it is concerned with the full project set.

This determination has two dimensions. The first part of preplanning is concerned with an analysis of the company's strategic posture in terms of strengths, weaknesses, and the ability of the firm to respond appropriately to opportunities and threats as they arise. The second part concentrates attention on identifying actions that can be taken to improve this strategic posture and render the company better able to capitalize on opportunities and to meet adverse contingencies.

Preplanning is an activity that is conducted at an overall company level. It is concerned with very broad but relevant considerations dealing with the ability of the firm as an entity to place itself in an advantageous position with respect to both capital and product markets. While the analysis may at times focus attention on subsets of the firm such as business units, business areas, resource areas, or influence areas, the evaluation criteria remain defined in terms of the subset's impact on the company as a whole.[2]

PREPLANNING AND CONVENTIONAL STRATEGIC PLANNING

There is a fundamental difference between preplanning as it is envisioned here and the conventional process of strategic planning.[3] To engage in planning, it must be assumed that reliable data are available to describe comprehensively both the environment and the influence of the means at the disposal of the firm to respond to its environment. In the absence of change or with rather slow evolution, management's assessment based on insights, experience, and available information is often reliable and sufficiently comprehensive for use in such planning. In this conventional process of strategic planning, it is implicitly assumed that management possesses the capability to estimate reliably for the planning period all relevant factors of particular importance to the analysis. In this context, it is also necessary for managers to know how to transform their subjective judgments regarding the future into trustworthy information that is adequate for use in the planning process.[4]

Under complex conditions of more rapid and less predictable change, however, the validity of extrapolations and other evaluations based mainly on historical information diminishes. When adequate, reliable data are not available to the company and it cannot be assumed reasonably that sufficient information can be acquired to be of use when decisions with potentially long-range impacts must be made, conventional planning is no longer strategically applicable. In this instance, the firm must start with preplanning.

The data requirements for preplanning are much less than for planning. Where traditional planning seeks to set in detail a course of action to meet a series of comprehensively perceived opportunities and threats, preplanning focuses on global guidance, based only on reliable information, for the broad development of the firm's capabilities. This enables the firm to influence, in an applicable and thus more flexible way, its own destiny. During the preplanning process, realistic inferences are drawn, considering complexity and dynamics, while refraining from planning if the perception on the basis of the available information is not sufficiently reliable. Developments that cannot be forecast are accepted as a fact of life, and attention is shifted to a preventive maintenance of the company's capabilities for dealing with the future.

The emphasis is directed to enhancing the general ability to survive shocks and to the timely development of resources to enable the company to seize as yet ill-identified, indistinct opportunities as they tend to arise. Thus preplanning also involves a search for broad capabilities to meet contingent threats and opportunities and includes, as a vital component, the concept of flexible response. The keys to effective preplanning are the maintenance of flexibility plus timely detection and proper interpretation of environmental signals to arrive at relevant guidance in highlights for the firm's strategic behavior.

Proper preplanning permits positioning the company in a strategically advantageous way for its stakeholders—all participants regarding the firm—compatible with topical flexibility. As more reliable information becomes available, the company can move from this global position into more specific planning and attain its strategic goals with less disruption than would otherwise be expected.

As the environment and the firm become more complex and the pace of change quickens, the quality of data available from all sources and, in particular, the timeliness of receipt tend to deteriorate rapidly. The number of possible influences that can have an impact—either favorable or unfavorable—on the well-being of the company increases dramatically. Even identifying the existence of opportunities or threats becomes much more difficult. In this situation, preplanning becomes quite important to promote the continued soundness of the firm.

THE NATURE OF THE FIRM AND ITS ENVIRONMENT

The corporation, as it has developed in the Western world, is both an economic and a legal entity.[5] In economic terms, its function of resource transformation or allocation is vital: resources in one form are acted upon to change their characteristics so that they are more useful to other entities. In this process, economic values, in principle, are created above those of the entering physical resources. The status of the firm as a legal entity is quite important in this respect. This status denotes that the company must conduct these operations subject to similar restrictions and limitations imposed on all other legal persons. That is, a corporation has an existence apart from that of the owners and thus carries corresponding social, political, and economic responsibilities that are borne by comparable members of the society. Such considerations serve as often-overlooked constraints on the ability of the firm to demand, over the long run, excessive remuneration for the benefit of one group (the owners) over the other members of the society, or, in principle, vice versa.

In performing the transformation function, the company interacts with its environment in terms of resource inputs, product or service outputs, and feedback information flowing in both directions. So that the company is successful and achieves fair compensation, the feedback information flowing from the firm's external setting must be perceived, correctly interpreted, and translated into an appropriate control response. This response will, in turn, transmit information to the environment, and the feedback and control loop will thus function.[6]

As the environment becomes more complex and subject to less predictable and greater change, the amount of feedback information increases. Consequently, at the same time that the volume is going up, there is a decrease in the available time in which the feedback information must be processed by the firm to be of use in preventing the development of undesirable structural tendencies. This leads to a deterioration of management's ability to distinguish the important feedback signals from the background noise soon enough to be of use in the planning process. One of the major problems faced by managers today is the inability to secure timely and relevant data for planning.[7] The evolution and consequences of this problem are particularly instructive for pointing the way toward its feasible relief.

PLANNING AND THE ENVIRONMENTAL CONTEXT

Historically a firm's executives could assume rather easily a reasonable value for external variables in a relatively stable or gradually evolving environment. Under this scenario, attention could be concentrated on the improvement of economic efficiency, and writers such as Frederick Taylor, Henri Fayol and Max Weber made important contributions to the advancement of this objective.[8] Elaborate schemes were developed by which the projects of the company could be chosen and managed, assuming the relatively stable external environment required by such a closed system approach.

By the 1960s, the consequences of environmental evolution had generated more interest in evaluating the impact of change on the firm. The major uncertainties of this era were economic or technological and mostly of a tangible nature. The period was characterized by increases in technology, the reentry into the world market of fierce competition, and the economic consequences of the collapse of colonial empires. Of major concern to management was the relevance of these tangible uncertainties for projects and their probability of occurrence.[9] There was not too much environmental complexity and a reasonable degree of stability regarding the general relationship between the company and the external world.

In the 1970s and particularly after the oil crisis of 1973, the issues of environmental complexity and changeability became paramount.[10] Cartel-type arrangements by the suppliers of raw materials, in several cases represented by government agencies, or the threat of such multinational arrangements, have led to less predictable movements and in some cases an aura of instability in world commodity markets. The breakdown of the Bretton Woods agreement has injected more instability into world money and capital markets. The large foreign exchange holdings of the OPEC nations and their potential for manipulating markets have become a serious problem. And the implications of militancy and the precarious economic position of many lesser developed countries must now be considered by internationally operating companies as fundamental components of their planning process. On top of this added complexity and change, a trend toward more governmental intervention in traditional areas of business decision making has led to additional difficulties for firms in responding to these challenges.

It is clear that environmental dynamics are becoming a much more significant issue today than they were in the past. The predictability of several important external variables such as the inflation rate and exchange rates has decreased. Similarly the importance of major unforeseen events, or "killer variables", has increased to the point that the likelihood of such an occurrence and a way to live with it must be considered explicitly.[11] In this context the emphasis is shifting even more toward explicit consideration of environmental tendencies.

The trend in management today is to concentrate attention on those variables that can be forecasted with reasonable reliability and to develop timely and built-in relevant capabilities to maintain the flexibility to respond as appropriate to that which at present is either ill identified or less foreseeable. The talk now is about strategic management rather than strategic planning.[12] Attention is shifting from long-range back to intermediate- and sometimes, albeit temporarily, even to the short-run perspective. This is supplemented with the promotion of capabilities to find applicable strategies and to ensure as far as possible the flexibility to act when opportunities of a perceived type arise and to cope with adverse contingencies.

Significantly this trend encourages the movement toward more preplanning as the logical starting place or initial identification phase in the decision process upon which all business activity is predicated. Because reaction time is becoming more limited, there is a need to conduct the strategic assessment process on a more frequent and regular basis, even before hard information is available in sufficient detail to engage in traditional planning. The main emphasis of preplanning is on managing increasing environmental complexity, but it also offers help in finding a way to live reasonably with moderate dynamics. In fact, preplanning, as developed in this book, is particularly useful for conducting a structured analysis of the strategic posture of the firm. It also stimulates paying timely attention to the relevant use of the limited amount of reliable information available today.

PREPLANNING AS A STEP TO BETTER PERFORMANCE

Preplanning is based on comparisons between the company in question and a carefully selected reference firm. This reference firm is chosen from the perspective of performance in both the product and the capital markets as a fundamentally sound and well-managed company. Thus it serves as a model of what the markets deem to be a sound-performing firm along the most salient strategic dimensions.

By anchoring the preplanning analysis to this known or knowable benchmark, value judgments of good and poor can be drawn when evaluating the own company. Such comparisons can give directional guidance to management and further situationally sound behavior when the analysis is conducted within an economically valid framework. However, the characteristics to be evaluated relative to the reference firm must be chosen carefully to promote sufficient insight into prominent strategic aspects.

Preplanning can be characterized as a typological approach to strategic posture assessment. The selected features to be evaluated relative to the reference firm are used to typify the current departure situation of the company. It is this situation that is subjected to analysis of strategic strengths and weaknesses and from which inferences are drawn for recommended changes in strategy. Departing from this overall situation, reflection is not only needed on a static balance between the main facets of the corporate strategy but must be given to the dynamic attributes of balanced behavior to ensure the continued well-being of the company.

In the perspective of environmental dynamics, both prospective analysis and monitoring of the firm's strategic posture should be done to further the extraction of relevant information. Prospective analysis, utilizing a "doing nothing strategically new" scenario, helps to reveal deficiencies in the current line of conduct and indicates what changes are necessary to improve the strategic position of the company.[13] Monitoring this posture promotes early detection of signs indicating future problems and thus facilitates timely countermeasures, if warranted, to place the company in the best possible position to meet the situational challenge.

Of crucial importance, preplanning promotes situationally sound and balanced behavior from the financial-strategic point of view. This ability is assured since the methodology to be presented has a foundation in and is developed from the financial economics theory for the valuation of the firm. By superimposing relevant strategic precepts on this foundation, a synthesis is achieved between financial economics and strategic management that is superior when compared with techniques developed solely within either discipline. Because of this synthesis, preplanning inhibits the tendency to make unjustified assumptions about data availability. Such often implicit suppositions tend to ignore the real issues of managerial action and may lead to elegant, but not infrequently misleading, "solutions" to strategic problems.

STRUCTURE OF THE BOOK

Chapter 2 introduces the concepts of strategic analysis to financial managers to show why inadequate attention to the pertinent considerations is conceptually wrong. In this chapter the Potential And Resilience Evaluation (PARE) method is explained.[14] PARE, used in conjunction with a properly specified departure situation, is the fundamental link between financial and management theories and serves as the backbone of the preplanning analysis.

Chapter 3 extends the developments of chapter 2 by demonstrating that the PARE method is able to define the cause-and-effect relationship between managerial actions and capital market reaction in a logical and pragmatically useful way. After discussion of problems regarding the firm's objective, a brief survey is given of existing managerial and financial techniques for planning. An examination of each in light of the developed theoretical framework shows that all are incomplete in one or more salient dimensions and thus can lead to unjustified generalizations.

The reasons for utilizing a typological approach to strategic analysis are given in chapter 4. The basics of finding a relevant characterization of the departure situation are then explained, and the groundwork is laid for the application examples that are presented later.

Chapter 5 expands upon the material presented in the first four chapters by showing typification steps used to structure the company's departure situation. As part of the discussion, the logic path is traced through the step-by-step typification of an example firm. It is shown in chapter 6 that situationally justified indications for strategic actions emerge from the analysis of this departure situation. Before this example can be examined in all relevant dimensions, the Balancing Identification Method (BIM) must be explained.[15] BIM is a tool both for structuring the strategic analysis and for the pertinent extraction of information to ensure that the forthcoming preplanning suggestions represent a well-proportioned strategy for the long-term behavior of the company. The focus of the last half of this chapter is on providing assistance for managing complexity by a balancing approach to the various considerations that play a strategic role in the preplanning process.

To this point, a general description of the preplanning methodology has been given and a specific example has been worked out. However, the real power of the typification method has still to be highlighted. This method is helpful in discriminating between situations that are, at first glance, only subtly different but that lead to widely diverging preplanning suggestions. It is the purpose of chapter 7 to demonstrate the ramifications of this discriminating power and, as a secondary consideration, to show why other techniques are unable to make these worthwhile distinctions.

The intention of the overall typification discussed so far is to discover broad but applicable recommendations for improving the strategic posture of the firm. To reflect on the specific measures needed for improvement, a follow-up in the form of additional typification steps may be useful. Implementation problems especially demand further typification since supplementary information is essential for extracting more elaborate recommendations for corrective action. Chapter 8 discusses this additional problem-oriented typification. As an illustration of the way in which problems that can be expected to profit from further typification are effectively dealt with, the "where" problem of internationalization is investigated.

Chapter 9 formally introduces the treatment of dynamics. Furthermore, it serves the purpose of injecting the time dimension more directly and explictly into the analysis via prospective tracking of the firm's project set. To facilitate tracking, or following the expected development over time of qualitative but strategically important characteristics, the Cardinal Ordering of Near-Intangible Characteristics (CONIC) approach is explained.[16] It is emphasized that tracking of the project set under review can and should be done both in terms of a "doing nothing strategically new" scenario and as an assessment of the expected impact of implementation problems with respect to recommendations for strategic improvement.

The book includes a comprehensive glossary of strategic characterization factors that have been utilized in the text. For each reference, these entries are presented in alphabetical order and contain essential information concerning definitions, reference points, and classification schemes. This glossary should be considered as a detailed extension of the text material to be used in conjunction with the specification of typification steps and the prospective tracking.

2 STRATEGIC FUNDAMENTALS FOR EFFECTIVE FINANCIAL MANAGEMENT

Financial management is of vital importance to form a close link between corporate management practices and the principles of economic theory. As finance has evolved over the last thirty years, more emphasis is being transferred to the economics side of the linkage as a foundation for examining business practices. In this way, procedures to increase the economic effectiveness and efficiency of management decision making can be recommended. Many important contributions and great insight have been realized by this development, but there also exists a danger that difficulties could arise.

Abstraction is required in developing economic theory and is also needed when financial concepts are derived. This is understandable since some degree of abstraction is usually necessary to enable one to come to grips with the central problem, but care must be taken to ensure that the substance of the problem situation is not eliminated by insubstantial concepts. Another danger is inherent in the possible abuse of abstraction by those less knowledgeable than the developers of the concepts. For instance, students—who, sometimes without acquiring direct business experience to put the concepts into the proper perspective, might become professors and pass on the concepts—may perceive the abstraction as the reality upon which other generalizations are based. This focus can distort the context of the decision process and invalidate the further developments as far as they are intended for actual use.

As explained in this chapter, there are reasons to believe that to a degree this perception or focus has happened with some financial models. The paucity of references to vital strategic concepts and, not infrequently, the heroic assumptions of data availability or estimateability open such financial modeling to the criticism that has been directed against it by businessmen. The foundation for the preplanning methodology developed in this book is the financial economic theories of valuation of the firm. Therefore, attention must be turned to validating these theories in the larger environmental context and extending them, where necessary, in situationally justified directions.

STRATEGY AND STRATEGIC ANALYSIS

Strategy is a word often encountered in the business world that can mean different things to different people. Thus, it is important for a book about project set strategies to make clear what is intended by the term. It can be defined as involving "the determination of the basic long-term goals and objectives and the adoption of courses of action and the allocation of resources necessary for carrying out these goals. . ."[17] It is "stated in such a way as to define what business the company is in or is to be in and the kind of company it is or is to be."[18]

Several points should be noted about this definition. First, strategy is a long-term concept. Exact specification of what time horizon is implied in this introductory description is not feasible because, for instance, what would be considered long range to a firm in the high-technology electronic components industry may be short term to a large electric utility company. In general, long range should be assumed to imply a period of time at least as long as the expected economic life of the major cash-flow-generating current activities of the firm.

Also contained in this definition is the idea that strategy involves determination of goals, adoption of courses of action to achieve them, and allocation of resources consistent with those actions. In finance, primary emphasis is given to the third aspect, allocation of resources, and it is usually assumed that the first two aspects are given. Attention is thus directed at achieving economic efficiency in the allocation of resources—in the sense of maximizing excess returns from projects—when all possible appropriations are implicitly assumed to be equally efficient in all other dimensions.

Furthermore, strategy must define the business that the company is in and what kind of company it is. By imposing these requirements on the firm under review, the number of feasible resource allocations is drastically curtailed. Just because General Motors may be able to earn the required rate of return on a project involving the construction of large computer systems—that is, the project has a positive net present value—does not necessarily mean that the investment should be made, even if there are no other current uses for the resources. Unless General Motors is willing to redefine itself to include being in the computer business, management is explicitly communicating that they perceive even greater but sometimes still indistinct opportunities for high return in the current lines of business, even when the resources are left temporarily idle. Thus strategy, as defined above, suggests that resource allocations should be made so as to enable the efficient implementation of the chosen courses of action to achieve clearly defined corporate objectives for the long run.

In ascertaining the degree of success management has enjoyed in making past allocations and for suggestions to improve future corporate performance, the strategic path of development should be kept in mind. To be valid, such analyses must be conducted within the overall strategic framework, where good performance along all applicable dimensions is the governing criterion, rather than in a context restricted by unjustified simplifying assumptions. With this in mind, attention can now be turned to strategic analysis and to why these concepts are important for the study of financial management.

Strategic analysis refers to the process of evaluating the continuing appropriateness of the strategic objectives, goals, courses of action, and resource allocations in the face of environmental complexities and dynamics. This suggests the importance of a feedback process whereby environmental signals can be perceived, correctly interpreted, and translated into an adequate control response.

If the current goals and courses of action remain strategically valid when evaluated in the perspective of the relevant problem situation, the control response will operate at the level of resource allocations. However, if the present courses of action are no longer appropriate, they must be revised to reflect the changed situation. At this point, the resource allocations have to be examined and adjustments or adaptations made to harmonize them with the new line of conduct. Similarly, if an alteration in the objectives is indicated, the control response should first focus on the next highest dimension of strategy and then work downward systematically.

Although not generally recognized as such, these ideas about strategy and strategic analysis are of great significance for the study of business finance. By its very nature, financial management is a process involving the commitment of large amounts of scarce resources. Before this allocation of resources can take place, it is necessary to identify what the company wishes to accomplish, what means the firm commands, where it is lacking in resources, and how this lack can be rectified. Correcting shortcomings and committing means efficiently requires that the main dimensions of the corporate strategy be taken into consideration. Indeed the allocation of resources is, by definition, an integral part of the larger strategic process.

In a dynamic environment, allocations must also be made while keeping in mind the flexibility to maneuver if and when future contingencies may dictate a change in the corporate strategy. Such changes may lead to a different pattern or other priorities of resource commitments, which in turn should be reflected in the allocation plan. For instance, the strategic decision to enter a promising new field of endeavor or to divest from an existing market will result in a diversion of means from one activity to another. This move can involve more than a shift in the pattern of asset allocation. If certain remaining activities in which the firm is engaged are more congruous than others to the market trend identified by management and used as the justification for changing the strategy, resources may be further concentrated in them, reflecting a change in the priorities of the overall allocation plan.

Thus the commitment of resources is an integral part of both financial management and the strategic process. Since strategy is a broader, more encompassing field than finance, financial models achieve validity only in the context of the overall strategic situation.

STRATEGIC PRACTICES IN FINANCIAL MANAGEMENT

At the present time, little attention is paid to operating procedures that include explicitly strategic considerations as an integral part of the resource planning and allocation process. Scenario planning and what if? sensitivity analysis, particularly when conducted within the context of a broad-scope company model, are aids for injecting strategic reflections into the asset planning process.[19] However, these and similar techniques—of unquestioned value for gaining insight into the difficult problems of environmental complexity and change—are not entirely adequate to inject strategic considerations into the analysis in the most useful way. Their main limitation is that they offer inadequately structured insight as to what investment types the firm should be considering. That is, they are of too little help in identifying project characteristics that should be sought to put the firm on a stronger competitive footing. They also have high data requirements that may sometimes be unreasonable in light of environmental complexity and change.

In fact, in the literature of finance, there is little mention of the strategic dimension of asset planning and selection. Most textbooks either ignore the issue altogether or devote only a few paragraphs to say that the capital budget should be consistent with the corporate strategy. A few books mention briefly the concept of strategy development within the firm as a lead-in to capital budgeting.[20] However, these discussions are superficial and usually boil down to the idea of narrowing the range of different types of projects in which the firm is interested.

This inadequate attention to strategic issues in resource allocation decisions is surprising since it is widely recognized in the finance literature that, in addition to working capital, fixed assets can have both a very strong short- and long-run impact on the financial condition of the firm. The timing patterns of cash requirements and cash throw-off by projects can affect the amount of liquidity, the unused borrowing capacity, and the ability of the company to react in the short term to opportunities or threats. In addition, the operating leverage consequences of a project can magnify cash needs or throw-offs with similar impact on the company.

Characteristics not related directly to cash flow but having important ramifications for the well-being of the firm have also been discussed in the financial literature. Of particular importance for the strategic dimension, various forms of resource rationing have been introduced in financial models.[21] These generally take the form of constraints on the supply of raw materials, skilled labor, time, or capital at the company's disposal. Unfortunately these rationing conditions have usually been treated as externally imposed constraints on the project selection process. While not within the stated purpose of these models (except, perhaps, in the case of capital), the strategic perspective would require thought as to how the limits can be overcome, if desirable, in the foreseeable future. This is true because, as Hastie points out, most companies operate almost continuously under some form of resource rationing that, depending upon several factors, both predictable and otherwise, can have serious consequences for the profitability and even the survival of the firm.[22]

Given the above considerations, it is likely that a misdirected asset planning and selection process has the latent ability to cause serious long- and short-term disequilibriums that can lead to financial stress. Environmental complexity is increasing, and there is more changeability of the firm's external context, making it harder to recognize influences that can lead to these disequilibriums—but timely identification of such situational factors remains an essential for sound management. Also, the cash-flow streams from different projects can be in or out of phase because of both statistical (correlation) and economic (timing, project life cycle) causes. For this reason, it is more difficult to assess the company-wide implications of environmental dynamics without systematic reflection on and balancing of the considerations mentioned above. These characteristics in the environmental perspective and their impact on the firm are at the heart of strategic analysis.

INTRODUCING STRATEGIC GUIDANCE BY PROJECT SET PREPLANNING

The nature of the business environment with greater complexity and change has encouraged the shift of early emphasis from planning to preplanning. Increasingly the problem encountered by management is lack of enough reliable data upon which comprehensive plans can be based. Even such techniques as scenario analysis are of little help since what may turn out to be, ex post, the most critical factor is often difficult to ascertain ex ante for use in setting elaborate plans.

An analysis of the current strategic posture of the firm is the appropriate platform upon which the development of the new project set can effectively be based. Thus it is advisable to start the preplanning process by giving consideration to this current posture. Additionally, starting from this departure point helps to guard against the analysis's leading to irrelevant generalizations.

The strategic posture of the company can be ascertained in a useful way through comparative analysis with an appropriately defined external benchmark or reference firm. Such a reference firm is a company, preferably of similar size and product mix and operating in the same industry(ies) or in a related activity field, that is classified as sound by the financial world in terms of the characteristics required not only to survive but to thrive in the environment under review.

This reference firm is used as a benchmark to facilitate a relative analysis of the strategic strengths and weaknesses of the company under study. Since, by definition, the financial world (market) has classified the reference firm as sound, analysis of relative strengths and weaknesses of a company along several dimensions can give management an idea of the strategic areas in which it needs to improve to become more attractive to the financial community. This analysis may also reveal areas of perhaps hidden strengths that can be exploited to achieve a better competitive position.

Using a carefully defined reference firm is better than relying on an arbitrary industry average for orientation since adequate similarity is vital for strategic comparisons—provided that the financial markets have passed judgment on the benchmark as a sound firm. Comparisons can also be made according to several essentially qualitative factors through an analysis relative to the reference firm, whereas such assessments would remain undefined using an industry average as a benchmark.

These strategic comparisons involve the explicit consideration of several environmental and internal variables with, as a by-effect, a tendency to increasing complexity. The definitions of strategy and strategic analysis indicate that an analysis in diverse perspectives is necessary to focus attention on the most salient facets of important strategic issues. Although individual relative comparisons are fairly easy to make in isolation, when considered together, it is rather difficult to structure them in a manner that ensures the extraction of the maximum amount of strategically significant and applicable information. Thus a structuring and summarizing device is required to reduce the complexity without destroying essential data.

This device should consolidate the information into a framework that is meaningful to management. In this way, the aggregated information portrayed by the summarizing factor(s) is stated in terms of concepts that can at once be identified with broad strategic attributes of paramount importance for developing the project set. The number of aggregating strategic factors should be kept at a minimum consistent with retention of the essential data contained in the individual comparisons.

POTENTIAL AND RESILIENCE EVALUATION OF THE FIRM'S PROJECT SET

Going back to the underlying financial economic theories of the valuation of the firm as expounded by Gordon or Modigliani and Miller, the present value of a company is a function of its cash-flow stream in perpetuity capitalized at a rate of return sufficient to induce investors to hold the stocks and bonds of the firm.[23] The perpetual cash-flow stream implies that the cash throw-off from the current project set is important, *but so is the ability of the firm to find and exploit profitable projects in the future.* The all-encompassing capitalization rate is designed to compensate investors for the variability of the cash flow, *as well as for another important component* that may be only indirectly linked with variability of cash flow: the chance that, for whatever reason, the firm will have to cease operations and liquidate, or, in other words, become bankrupt. The PARE method is consistent with and follows directly from the above considerations with respect to the valuation of the firm.

To assess the company's capability to attain its strategic objectives a corporate planner focuses attention in the first instance on the Potential of the firm. *Potential* refers to the ability of the company to generate and utilize attractive return possibilities for both the present and the future.

Opportunities is the designation given to projects that possess Potential. The existence of opportunities gives a primary indication of the ability of the firm to remain competitive in the marketplace. Adequate opportunities are also an essential determinant of the market value of the company. Hence, opportunities is the first Strategic Element identified as important for project set development.

According to the valuation models mentioned above, identification of opportunities is necessary but not sufficient to describe the Potential of the firm in an appropriate way. A parallel consideration is the likelihood that such opportunities can be feasibly exploited by the company as deemed advisable. This involves a determination of whether the firm has the resources readily available for use in exploiting the opportunities according to its strategic plans. This capability to act is referred to as the *action range* and depends not only on the company's financial competence but also on available managerial talent, manpower, technical and marketing expertise, and organizational and logistical flexibility. Without the capability to exploit opportunities in a timely manner, the Potential of the firm cannot be realized. Hence, action range is the second strategic element identified as important for project set preplanning. By considering both opportunities and action range together in the form of Potential, a richer concept that is more consistent with the theories of valuation than "return" emerges.

An evaluation of the Potential of the company under review is based on the planner's assessment of the two strategic elements for Potential—opportunities and action range—relative to the reference firm. These two elements are distinguishable but not separable in evaluating the corporate Potential. In the preparatory phase of the strategic evaluation process, explicit attention to these factors in the indicated order is essential. During this process, management will have to combine its assessments of opportunities and action range to arrive at a strategically meaningful identification of the company's Potential relative to the reference firm. Without explicit attention to these strategic elements—opportunities and then action range—during this crucial phase, the danger of an uncritical lumping together is too manifest.

In the second instance, the company's ability to withstand environmental threats and hold steady in the face of unfavorable contingencies has to be identified. This protective ability of the firm to cope with adversities associated with its projects, to handle contingencies, and to recoup to its original, if not to a better, position for future action is referred to as the corporate *Resilience.*

The first key determinant of Resilience is the uncertainty to which the relevant cash flows are exposed in the sense that the realized return from the investments may be less than the expected return. This, the third strategic element, is referred to as the *risk* of the company and is approached through management's assessment of the variability and sensitivity of the firm's cash flow to contingent setbacks. However, risk alone is not sufficient to describe adequately the concept of Resilience. A parallel consideration to risk is the capability of the company to marshal resources to ensure survival in the event of adverse developments. This is referred to as the firm's *endurance* and is the fourth important strategic element.

The probability of a very low cash-flow outcome is not a sufficient indication of "bankruptcy risk" except in a ceteris paribus sense. This is true since suffering an extremely low cash-flow outcome at a time when endurance is high may have less serious bankruptcy implications than the occurrence of a "better" or higher cash-flow outcome when endurance is very low. Endurance thus refers to the company's capability to cope with unfavorable contingencies when beset with difficulties.

An evaluation of the Resilience of a company is based upon the planner's assessments of the two strategic elements for Resilience—risk and endurance—relative to the reference firm. It is important to imagine that in evaluating the corporate Resilience, risk and endurance are distinguishable but not separable.

To determine in a strategically meaningful way the company's Resilience in comparison to the reference firm, management's relative assessments of risk and endurance will have to be combined. During this important reflection phase, the danger of an uncritical consolidation is manifest without an adequate preparation by explicitly paying attention to these strategic elements in the correct order: risk and then endurance.

Resilience as determined in this way is consistent with the valuation theory concept that underlies—or requires compensation for an investor to endure—the determination of the capitalization rate. It incorporates the idea of the variability or the distribution of possible cash-flow outcomes, including the likelihood of low values. Also, it includes a consideration of the resources and capabilities that the company can marshal to offset or overcome adverse cash flow. Thus both components of bankruptcy risk are explicitly taken into account.

Just as the four strategic elements were condensed into two comprehensive components or Key Strategic Factors—Potential and Resilience—that reflect the underlying information in main lines, it is desirable to compress further the information into a single survey of the strategic posture of the company relative to the reference firm. Condensing the information into a single or grand indicator facilitates directional guidance for assessing the company's posture. In this way, the firm's overall attractiveness is also considered according to the financial markets in which the leading investment banks are of particular relevance from the corporate point of view.

This grand indication can be achieved by use of the comparative analysis or PARE chart for classification as shown in figure 2-1. The chart has only two positions—strong and weak—for each Key Strategic Factor. However, a similar posture should also be permitted in a relative analysis. Such position can be plotted on the solid line that separates the cells of the chart, thus preserving directional indications for improvement. If either of the company's Key Strategic Factors is similar to the reference firm's, any strategic issues in that perspective will not be so prominent, so attention is focused mainly on the more salient postures.

Note that the reference firm plots in the center of the chart by this convention. Thus, PARE position I dominates the reference firm, PARE positition IV is

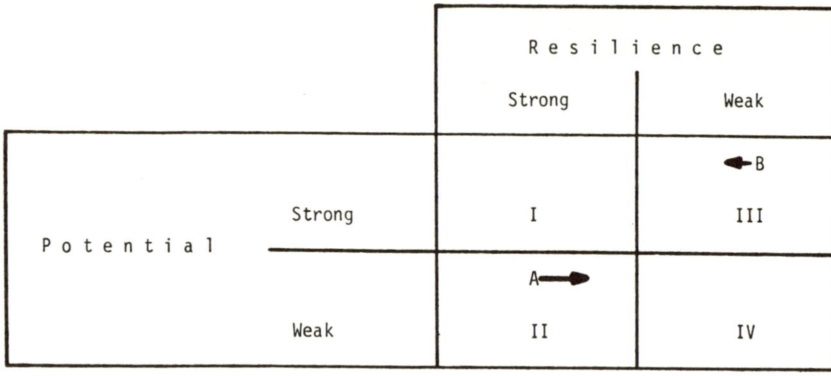

Figure 2-1. PARE or Comparative Analysis Chart

dominated by the reference firm, and for PARE positions II and III there are mixed indications (but for different causes).

It is also possible to indicate further strategically significant information on the PARE chart. Since business is a dynamic undertaking, a prospective reflection on the evolution of the company's PARE position over the planning period is vital. In the context of a doing-nothing-strategically-new scenario, where the firm is assumed to maintain its present strategy unchanged, the direction of movement of the PARE position can be ascertained as an auxiliary indication. This is marked on the PARE chart by a directed arrow, the length of which is a function of the perceived speed of the movement.

Such auxiliary indications are also displayed in figure 2-1. Firm A is currently in PARE position II, but the scenario analysis indicates that there is a tendency to drift at a moderate rate toward PARE IV because of a deteriorating Resilience position. On the other hand, company B is now in PARE position III, but actions taken to improve the Resilience are slowly taking effect to move the firm toward PARE I.

A prospective analysis approach such as this can indicate the appropriateness of the current strategy against the background of the company's objectives. Based on the doing-nothing-strategically-new scenario, it will be useful to reflect upon possible deviations from the desired path of development by the expected movement of the PARE position. A gap between the desired and expected positions would focus attention on changes that need to be made to render the strategy more appropriate for the future. In this way, this scenario analysis aids in the discovery process to find strategically justified conclusions and relevant recommendations for action.

PARE AS A TOOL FOR FINANCIAL MANAGEMENT

Potential and Resilience are richer than and conceptually closer to the ideas underlying the Gordon and Modigliani-Miller valuation methodologies than the generally recognized measures of return and risk. On the level of the firm, the growth rate of the cash flow utilized in the valuation models can be considered, in principle, to be compatible with the concepts of opportunities and action range. However, this global measure is not intended to give information on these elementary concepts. Therefore, it does not provide guidance about how to make decisions that promote a proper balance among the strategic elements. In other words, the cash-flow growth rate is a variety-starved indicator that violates Ashby's law of requisite variety.[24] Similarly for the capitalization rate, *k*, on the level of the firm, the effects of strategic elements such as risk and endurance are compressed into a single indicator without adequate differentiation possibilities and so with inadequate variety.

On the level of the project, return represents a myopic calculation that considers only the timing and the magnitude of the cash flow, thus ignoring other dimensions of the problem, such as the impact of the project on future opportunities, action range, risk, and endurance. The discount rate for a project can only be properly defined with respect to the contribution by the project to all of the strategic elements as evaluated at the level of the company. "Risk" in isolation is an inadequate concept when defined in terms of, for example, variance of cash flow, semivariance, and probability of loss, unless certain assumptions are made. In isolation, risk is an appropriate measure if and only if it can reasonably be assumed that any imbalance or other problems in the perspective of the four strategic elements either vanish or are, at a minimum, compensated for. In the way that risk is usually employed, this implies that "adequate" compensation is achieved when the cash-flow rate of return, calculated by a rather mechanical procedure, is at least as high as the cutoff rate *determined as a function of risk alone.* It is unrealistic, however, to assume problems away or to think that they are automaticlaly compensated for when completely ignored in calculating the discount rate.

Since the PARE approach is richer in variety than the conventional measures of return and risk, and it is indeed in harmony with the long-run concepts that are the basis for valuation of the firm, it should prove to be useful as a tool for financial managers. In the PARE method, dimensions of the business environment that practitioners have identified as important for financial decisions are considered explicitly.[25] Also, this method is consistent with the thrust of academic thinking on simulation and goal programming as to the need for multi-aspect criteria for financial decision making.[26]

To introduce sufficient structure for conducting a PARE analysis, it is important to base the comparisons on a typological approach to the firm's departure situation. The typification steps should be selected to shed enough light on all of the four strategic elements to reveal the PARE position of the company with a minimum amount of ambiguity. This comparative assessment of the PARE position permits a market-anchored determination of the strategic posture of the firm and can give useful signals about possibly hidden strengths and weaknesses long before their existence or implications are manifest.

Suggestions based on the PARE analysis for actions to take to exploit opportunities, to defend against threats, or other ways to strengthen the posture of the company should result in a comprehensive, overall strategy. One can evaluate the project set with respect to the four strategic elements by reflecting on the implications of the recommendations in the PARE perspective. Using these reflections, preplanning suggestions can be derived that contribute to an increase in Potential, Resilience, or both, while not decreasing either.

BIM can also be of help in this respect by aiding the balancing of various pairs of desirable but sometimes contrasting strategic considerations. By reflecting systematically on these long-term considerations that are often difficult to reconcile, BIM can provide guidance on how to search for efficiently balanced combinations of actions that, taken together, will meet the strategic needs of the situation. Thus, a PARE analysis, supplemented by BIM insights, can provide strategically applicable information. Such evidence is helpful in preparing business decisions, including those usually associated with financial management, so that relevant recommendations for actions can be found.

3 THE BASIS FOR ADEQUATE PREPLANNING

Potential and Resilience as concepts are, in principle, more comprehensive than return and risk as used in the conventional sense. The discussion about these concepts can be expanded to serve as a basis for linking managerial actions to market reactions. By establishing this linkage in a way that is both theoretically supportable and meaningful to managers, preplanning from the PARE perspective is a powerful tool for launching the resource allocation process in the right direction.

POTENTIAL AND RESILIENCE AS DETERMINANTS OF VALUE

Both Potential and return are functions of the cash flow of the firm in perpetuity. However, return assumes as data some expected cash flow over time, often stated in terms of a present or known amount and an expected growth rate. It assumes further that management will take whatever actions are necessary to achieve this cash-flow stream, although in no place are these actions identified explicitly. Thus it is valid to say that return specifies the effect and tends to ignore the cause(s).

In contrast, Potential focuses primary attention not on the cash flow as an exact numerical amount but rather on the characteristics of the firm that will result in or cause a good value for the cash flow. Only if these characteristics are present to a sufficiently large degree will the cash-flow value be acceptably high. However, relatively greater differentiation is possible since Potential can be decomposed into the strategic elements of opportunities and action range.

The concept of opportunities is of both a short- and a long-run nature. In this respect, the future impact of current decisions on the ability of the firm to generate profitable returns and to exploit project cash flows is specifically considered. Action range, or the capability to exploit opportunities as they arise, needs to be made explicit as a constraint on the ability of the firm to generate future cash flows. By explicit consideration of these parallel concepts, a more structured and refined analysis is possible. In doing so, there is less chance for unjustified generalizations or arbitrary projections of current circumstances.

Opportunities and action range together are broader and more comprehensive than the idea of return. This implies that it is more difficult to derive a simple numerical representation for them in the way that a calculation of return can be made. No problems are presented by this, however, since a capital market-validated benchmark can be identified from which directed guidance is possible through relative comparisons. The comparisons tend to focus attention on managerial actions and their impact on the ability of the firm to generate and capitalize on opportunities. For making resource allocation decisions, this focus is most valuable. Potential has greater utility for accomplishing this than the conventionally defined concept of return.

On the other side of the coin, there is also a fundamental difference between the PARE concept of Resilience and the traditional concept of risk. Even though there is wide disagreement about the exact definition of risk in the traditional sense, most measures are defined in terms of the statistical properties of variability or covariability of the project's cash flow. Other measures of risk, such as that associated with the capital asset pricing model (CAPM), concentrate attention not on the cash flow but directly on the variability or covariability of the firm's stock return, which results from the market evaluation of the company's cash-flow characteristics.

The conventional measures of risk, based upon such statistical definitions, assume implicitly that there is a direct cause-effect relationship, without other intervening factors, between probability of loss in the cash-flow sense and risk of bankruptcy. This assumption has been shown to be questionable since endurance clearly has an important role in determining the risk of bankruptcy. It should be noted that the underlying theories of valuation, which are generally recognized as theoretically sound, neither assume nor require this relationship since they simply define a capitalization rate sufficient to compensate investors for the risk (broadly perceived) inherent in the cash-flow stream of the firm. Not surprisingly, in attempts to implement these theories in practice, difficulties arise in measuring risk. These problems materialize when trying to identify a single figure of demerit that captures all relevant dimensions of the problem.

Resilience differs from the conventional approach in that it includes two relevant aspects that in principle interact to determine this risk-compensated capitalization rate. The strategic element labeled risk very closely follows the usual (non-CAPM) definitions of risk. Endurance supplements the measure of risk by introducing different overall firm characteristics that add another dimension to the determination of the likelihood of bankruptcy or other situations of financial stress. Thus Resilience defined by the twin concepts of risk and endurance is more comprehensive and closer to the underlying theories of valuation than risk in isolation.

Both risk and endurance (as defined in this book) are, considering their nature and function, also difficult to quantify meaningfully in terms of a single figure. But this is of no real consequence since it can be overcome similarly as for Potential through relative comparisons anchored to a capital market-validated benchmark or reference firm. Implicit in this process is a strong assumption that in making resource allocation decisions, it is necessary to focus attention at the microfirm level on managerial actions and their implications mainly in the capital and product markets, but also within the organization and society as a whole.

Clearly there exist rather fundamental differences between return in the conventional sense and Potential on the one hand and risk in the usual sense and Resilience on the other. Potential and Resilience are in principle more compatible with the equivalent concepts in the underlying theories of valuation. For this reason, several simplifying but unrealistic assumptions would be required if one is to utilize the traditional measures of return and risk for purposes of preplanning the company's project set.

On the return side, it must for this purpose be presumed that the expected cash flow is defined to include the cash flow from all current and future projects exploited by the firm. This presumption implies that future opportunities will not only be defined but also that management will take appropriate and timely (although unspecified) action to generate the opportunities. Another implicit assumption is that the firm will possess the capabilities to exploit the opportunities as they arise—although no thought is given to how these abilities are identified and acquired.

On the risk side, it must be supposed that statistical measures of the dispersion of the distribution of cash flow from operations are adequate to capture all relevant dimensions of the risk (broadly perceived) for which investors demand a compensating premium. This implies constant endurance so that there is a direct linkage between probability of a low cash-flow outcome and the likelihood of bankruptcy. Beta as a risk measure for corporate project set preplanning is of little utility for two reasons. First, it is primarily intended for other purposes and is not defined in terms of the variables over which management has control to promote good performance of the firm. Second, the shareholders are not the only group to whom the firm has a moral obligation.

Corporate risk, as distinguished from capital market or beta risk, is important to these other groups and should also enter the project set selection process. If ignored, corporate risk can result in psychological and sociological aberrations that in the aggregation can have adverse capital market impacts. For instance, the decision not to build a supersonic transport had a strong impact on the whole American economy even though Boeing in Seattle was affected directly with this corporate risk. Thus for guidance in preplanning or managerial decision making, corporate risk in the context of Resilience is a much more useful tool than conventional risk.

Preplanning is an essentially entrepreneurial activity. It is a strategic fact of life inherent in any entrepreneurial activity that if one talks about managerial actions, one cannot at the same time assume away intrinsic problems. The simplified assumptions embodied in the conventional measures of return and risk conceal many of the crucial business problems and market imperfections. The function of an entrepreneur is to exploit the implications of such problems and imperfections, so they cannot be effectively assumed away. In fact, they play a central role in the preplanning and planning process.

It would be rather difficult to derive reliable quantitative measures for each of the strategic elements considering the applicable complexity and changeability. However, it is possible and useful to ascertain the effect of managerial actions on each element with respect to the direction and maybe even the rough magnitude of the impact. Actions taken to change one strategic element can have secondary ramifications on any or all of the other strategic elements. The cumulative effect of managerial actions, as reflected in relative changes in the mix of the four strategic elements (vis-à-vis the reference firm), determines the comparative shift in the Potential and Resilience of the company under review. These changes in the PARE position are in principle reflected in alterations in the market value of the firm as per the financial valuation models. A linkage between management actions and changes in the value of the firm has thus been established: managerial actions result in changes in at least one of the four strategic elements. Alterations in the strategic elements result in a different evaluation of Potential and Resilience. Changes in Potential and/or Resilience are reflected in a revision of the market value of the firm, especially in the long run.

ACTION GOALS AND GOOD PERFORMANCE

To ensure that the analytical framework for strategically augmented project set preplanning is sound, it is necessary at this point to determine a realistic and tangible overall objective toward which all decisions and activities of the firm can be directed. All effective behavior is, at least intrinsically, goal directed. An explicit elucidation of the objective of the firm promotes both deliberate consideration of alternatives and greater consistency and direction of effort by all divisions and individuals in the company.

It is a fundamental precept of performance evaluation to judge actual performance against the same predetermined standards used to establish required performance. However, required behavior can be defined with enough meaning in today's difficult circumstances only through specification of known or established reference points. Thus care must be exercised in choosing an objective for the firm to verify that such a reference point or benchmark can be reliably ascertained.

Much attention has been devoted in the literature of finance and management to the existence of multiple goals and the appropriateness of an assumed single objective function for analytical simplification. Inherent conflicts exist between the different stakeholders that play a role in the decision-making activities and operations of the corporation. The finance literature usually presumes that the interests of the shareholders very clearly predominate. However, other interest groups such as the directors, executives, employees, suppliers, customers, local communities, and even society as a whole have a stake in the continued existence and prosperity of the company. Not infrequently what is perceived to be in the best interests of the shareholders can be at variance with, for instance, society as a whole. Thus the firm is confronted with the task of balancing these conflicts of interest in setting its objectives.

It should be obvious that the stakeholder groups will not have equal weight or influence in defining the objectives to be pursued. For instance, the desires of equity holders are usually considered to have a higher priority than those of other stakeholders. Several concerns may be described equally well as threshold constraints rather than as goals. Other interests can be viewed as part of a means-ends chain where there is an overall guiding objective. Some goals are compatible, and others are inherently contrasting or even contradictory. Although no general statement about their composition is possible, two broad but distinct classes of often compatible, sometimes contrasting, and occasionally contradictory goals appear to develop: goals that inherently promote profit or economic value maximization and all other goals, often said to include such desirabilities as employee welfare and social responsibility—two goals of unquestionable importance in the business environment of today.

Given these two broad classes of goals that appear to coexist, it is reasonable in the preplanning context to define the prime objective of the firm in terms of only one of the classes—long-run economic value maximization—and incorporate the other class in the form of constraints. On this basis, there will exist a sound approximation of a benchmark for directional guidance. The economic reaction to managerial actions can be ascertained by observing the longer-term capital market reaction as it unfolds with respect to the stock price trend and the willingness and terms for acquiring new capital from external sources. This stock price trend will be assessed with respect to the relevant tendency in the past and the trend for other stocks.

There is no broadly based external indicator of social success with comparable explanatory power. However, some social elements are inherently imbedded in the economic indicator, or economic achievement is a prerequisite for their validity. Reflecting on the economic performance that is perceived by management to be the "best" obtainable, deviations for social desirabilities can then be investigated and the pertinent economic cost ascertained. Whether this economic cost is justified by the social benefits received is an executive decision.

Even if multiple goals with distinct external benchmarks could be developed, a similar type of trade-off function between economic cost and social benefit would have to be utilized to judge the ultimate allocation of resources. Thus it appears that judicious interpretation of the economic impact in the capital markets of managerial actions can function as an overall guiding objective when suitable constraints are taken into account. For the intended purpose, this constrained objective function is a sufficiently close and reasonable proxy for approaching comprehensive multiple goals.

An appropriate standard for action must now be specified against which it is possible to evaluate the economic impact in the capital markets of managerial actions. Economic theory suggests that maximizing the total market value of the firm in the long run is the proper goal for the company to adopt. This objective also includes some elements of social worth, such as the efficient allocation of scarce resources. There are difficulties, however, in establishing linkages between individual actions and changes in the stock price.

The major problem is that there is extraneous noise in the market system that tends to overwhelm the impact of managerial actions in the short run. To filter out as much of this noise as possible, the current strategic posture of the firm can be used as a point of reference. Any action that strengthens the strategic posture should, in principle, increase the long-run market value of the firm. Determining the direction of the economic impact is sometimes difficult but nearly always possible.

Another difficulty with stock price maximization is the implied availability of data. Maximization implies knowledge of the outcomes of all relevant variables, which is clearly impossible in practice. Instead of maximizing, management will use a satisficing approach to achieve a "sufficient" market value, both in terms of direction of change and a rough magnitude of change.

For the period in question, management will implicitly or explicitly establish a series of subgoals as steps in the right direction. It is realistic and particularly useful to assume that managerial actions affect some or all of the four strategic elements. It is the relative change in these elements that forms the link with changes in the firm's performance and, consequently, in the stock price.

These subgoals can be thought of as threshold values for the four strategic elements, the achievement of which will, in the opinion of management, result in a "satisfactory" market evaluation. Of course, this judgment is based on management's perception of the linkage between the firm's posture regarding the strategic elements and the long-run capital market reaction. Based on this set of subgoals, linkages between managerial actions and the impact on the strategic elements are determined by management reflection. The type and level of managerial action required to meet the satisficing economic objective can thus be estimated.

The satisficing subgoals, based on the four strategic elements, are linked to the concept of value maximization in economic theory by the market indications perceived by management to result, considering the likely reaction by the financial community, from changes in the variables under at least partial control by management. Given the purpose intended, this represents a usable link between management actions and capital market reaction that is of sufficient directional value. The circle is now complete since it has been shown that it is possible to ascertain this practical and theoretically supportable approach to the cause-effect relationship between managerial actions and changes in the value of the firm.

The leading finance literature in this respect, although not specifying the four strategic elements per se as important determinants of appropriate actions, is nonetheless compatible with the developed approach. For instance, the reasoning supporting simulation models and goal programs can be interpreted in terms of the necessity to balance the four strategic elements. Also, the relevant literature on financial planning that stresses the maintenance of flexibility and liquidity is also consonant with the need to consider explicitly action range and endurance.

PARE and the PARE-based analytical methodology is anchored to an intersubjective reference point outside and independent of the context of the characteristics being evaluated. This benchmark possesses the property of being able to give directed guidance through the representation of an overall position that can be determined as sound. Thus the PARE-based methodology is theoretically supportable and practically useful for preplanning the project set of a company.

Corporate Portfolio Techniques for Strategic Guidance

Several techniques for surveying the corporate project set are currently in use. Since these techniques differ somewhat dramatically from the methodology described thus far, a sharp contrast will be apparent. Throughout the rest of the book as the PARE-based methodology is developed, reference will be made to these other techniques to demonstrate why, although useful in other aspects, they tend to be inadequate in today's complex and changing environment.

The major trend toward diversification, both by product line and geographically, that started in the late 1950s spawned a new phenomenon in the business world: the multiproduct, multimarket conglomerate enterprise. While operating problems in managing these multiunit corporations could be eased by decentralization, the problem of strategic planning in a radically changing environment developed as a difficult new task for central management. Several techniques were developed by companies and outside consultants to cope with this new problem. All of these techniques have in common a view of the corporation as a portfolio of individual businesses. Thus they will be referred to collectively as *corporate portfolio techniques.*

The best known of the portfolio techniques that are frequently used today by multibusiness corporations is the share/growth matrix popularized by the Boston Consulting Group (BCG).[27] In this method, a business is defined as the smallest unit of a company for which strategic decisions can be made. The generation and use of cash by each of a firm's businesses are taken as distinctive measures for classification. According to the following logic, market share and market growth are the two variables chosen by BCG to reflect the cash-flow characteristics.

Under conditions of effective competition, the largest competitor in a market should be able to produce at the lowest cost. This is based on the underlying assumption of the BCG approach that the learning theory is valid. This theory predicts that unit costs decline as the rate of production increases. In addition to this learning-curve effect, scale advantages have an impact in the same direction. BCG concluded that market share is the major determinant of cash generation and captures this dimension.

Cash utilization in a business is presumed to be highly dependent on the growth rate of the market in which it operates. In fast-growing markets, heavy investment is needed just to maintain a constant market share. By attributing two possible values, high and low, to both cash-flow determinants—market share and market growth relative to their appropriate reference points—each business can be positioned on a 2X2 matrix, as illustrated in figure 3-1.

Each category in the share/growth matrix has its own characteristics. Because of their high growth rates, those with high growth and high share (referred to as *stars*) need large amounts of cash to maintain their leading position. On the other hand, their high market share promises a large amount of generated cash, though often predominantly in the long run. As a result, stars can be characterized as growth businesses with above-average return and moderate and, in time, rapidly declining cash requirements.

Market-Growth			
	High	"Star"	"Question Mark"
	Low	"Cash Cow"	"Dog"
		High	Low
		Market-Share	

Figure 3-1. The Share/Growth Matrix of BCG

In funds-generation terms, *cash cow* (low growth, high share) is in the short run the most favorable position for a business to be in. Low costs and a dominant position in a mature market lead to moderate profits and a large cash generation. Cash cows form the financial foundation of a company.

Even though cash requirements for *dogs* (low growth, low share) are low, cash generation will not normally suffice to balance those requirements. In very special and unique circumstances, such a business may be viable in a niche in the market, but usually it should be divested because of its unrewarding return.

High cash needs because of their high market growth and low cash generation resulting from their small market share make *question marks* highly cash absorbent. If risk is not too high and sufficient support is given, such businesses could become stars and then cash cows as they mature. On the other hand, question marks could turn into dogs, particularly if this support is neglected or omitted.

By depicting all individual businesses in the growth/share matrix, management gets a picture of the cash-flow characteristics of the current portfolio. From this overview, they can devise a strategy aimed at balancing the portfolio in the cash-flow perspective. There should be enough cash cows to generate cash. These funds are used to promote a carefully selected number of question marks, to support non-self-sustaining stars, and to liquidate dogs. By recognizing the portfolio role of each business, the general recommendation, according to BCG, is that cash cows should consolidate their favorable position without big reinvestments, stars should try to retain their leading position, question marks should quit or be doubled, and dogs should be eliminated.

Several other portfolio techniques have been developed utilizing the same principle of plotting businesses on a grid. Most of them incorporate a richer mix of variables in their portfolio positioning and thus are more sophisticated. Nevertheless, businesses are classified according to only two, although multifactorial, dimensions. These dimensions invariably refer to the attractiveness of the market in which a business operates and to the relative competitive strength that it enjoys. These may be regarded as more comprehensive substitutes for growth and share respectively. As a matter of fact, market share and market growth are among the factors that make up the two dimensions.

A further advantage is gained by attributing an intermediate position to both dimensions. This reduces the sharpness of the share/growth matrix, which may be misleading in practice. It permits a more refined positioning and more differentiated recommendations. Typical examples of these extended portfolio techniques are the ones developed by General Electric[28] and the Royal Dutch Shell Group.[29] Figure 3-2 depicts Shell's directional policy matrix, which has been mirrored to make it comparable to the share/growth matrix.

Several authors have pointed out some problems in the applications of corporate portfolio techniques.[30] Invariably they mention market definition and the segmentation of the corporation into business units. A business unit may hold a strong position within a small geographic area or in a specific market segment but may be rather weak in a more broadly defined market. On the other hand, if a business unit is defined too narrowly, learning and scale advantages will not come to light, and an overly pessimistic view of market position may be the result. Moreover, there is the problem of a possible discongruency between the real organization structure and the desired segmentation into business units, making the fundamental process of defining a company's businesses a very delicate problem that needs careful treatment in practice.

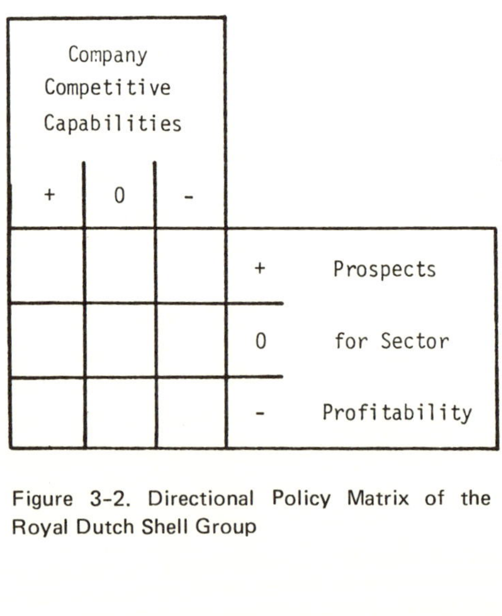

Figure 3-2. Directional Policy Matrix of the Royal Dutch Shell Group

An important advantage of the 2X2 share/growth diagram over the more sophisticated 3X3 matrices is its relative simplicity with respect to the information needed. Also, no arbitrary weighting of numerous variables is needed. But if portfolio analysis is restricted to market share and market growth, these factors should be reliably representative of company strength and market attractiveness, respectively. Recent empirical studies have indeed shown market share to be the major determinant of profitability.[31] However, the same studies also demonstrate that there are several other factors, such as investment intensity, that are of almost equal importance.

Market growth as an indicator for attractiveness could be very misleading in practice, as has been graphically shown by Ansoff and Leontiades.[32] In their portfolio model, market growth has therefore been replaced by life-cycle position. Four stages can be discerned—emergence, growth, maturity, and decline—to permit a more refined analysis. Although it may be difficult to determine reliably the position of a product in its life cycle, the replacement of market growth by life-cycle stage is a distinct improvement.

Lorange argues that portfolio techniques fail to take into account interbusiness relationships.[33] He advocates the addition of a third dimension to the matrix: consolidation attractiveness. As shown in figure 3-3, in this dimension synergy variables, as well as cash-flow characteristics, are incorporated. To elucidate this last inclusion, he states that a firm that has balanced its portfolio in the cash-flow perspective might still face liquidity problems if the timing of the generation and utilization of cash is out of phase. Furthermore, the portfolio analysis should include a study of the relative dependence of the firm's cash-generating potential upon its individual businesses.

The last criticism to be discussed is that of Pethia and Saïas.[34] They state that the current portfolio techniques are "not well-adapted to conditions of high complexity and instability." Indeed these methods draw insufficient attention to environmental aspects, an important omission in present times. Pethia and Saïas suggest the use of an additional matrix to offer some help with this problem. The axes of this additional diagram are labeled *complexity* and *instability*, and the firm's business units are situated according to their attributes in those respects. In this way, management gets a graphic representation of these considerations with which it has to cope.

Possibilities and Limitations of Portfolio Techniques in Preplanning

Preplanning can be regarded as the analysis of the strategic posture of the company to determine strengths and weaknesses therein. Four strategic elements need to be analyzed in preplanning: opportunities, action range, risk, and

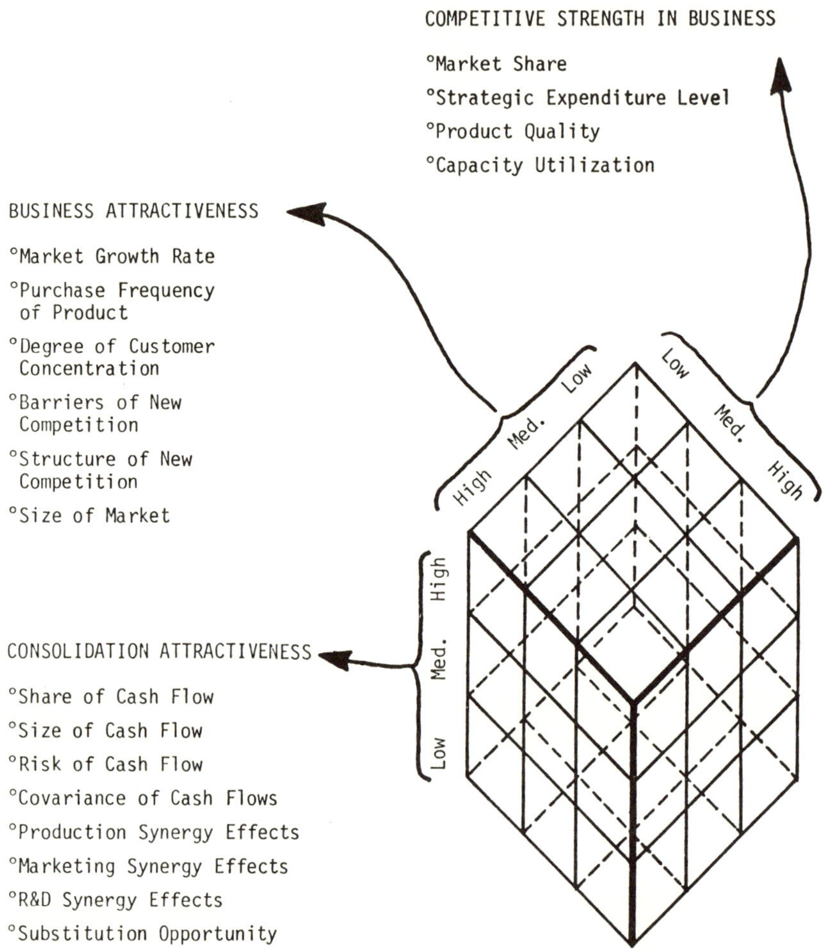

Figure 3-3. Matrix Determination and Evaluation of Business Line Product Strategy (Lorange)

endurance. Portfolio techniques draw particular attention to the attractiveness of investment opportunities and, as such, can be very useful in assessing the opportunities position of the firm. With respect to action range, these techniques are limited to cash-flow resources. In present times of high inflation, cash flow may indeed be the major constraint on a firm's action range, but other company capabilities such as expertise, skilled labor, continued availability of raw materials, and organizational and logistic flexibility should not be neglected.

In the portfolio techniques, risk and endurance are not dealt with adequately. The lack of sufficient attention to these strategic elements, making up the Resilience side of the firm's posture, is the most important deficiency of these techniques. To what disasters this omission may lead is clearly demonstrated by the examples cited by Fruhan in discussing points that should be given attention before starting a program for market share gain.[35]

Given all of the problems and shortcomings, portfolio techniques are at best incomplete for preplanning since they are too limited. They deal only with a partial analysis of the firm's departure situation so their recommendations may be based on unjustified generalizations. This is why, for preplanning purposes, these techniques must be placed in a broader context and supplemented by using other methods, such as the one presented in this book.

4 SITUATIONAL TYPIFICATION AS A STRATEGIC AID

The key to a methodology by which a preplanning analysis can be implemented under realistic business conditions is a typological approach to the identification of the current strategic posture of the firm. In this respect the PARE method, suitably extended, is particularly adept. In this chapter, the required extensions to PARE, such as expanded PARE-chart indications and interdependency enhancement of the PARE analysis, are developed. These extensions serve as the lead-in to the methodology for effective typification of a company's departure situation.

EXPANDED PARE-CHART INDICATIONS

The Potential And Resilience Evaluation method (PARE) is a powerful identification tool that can provide help in assessing the strategic posture of a company relative to an appropriate reference firm. Potential is analyzed with respect to the joint characteristics arising from an evaluation of opportunities and action range. Resilience is ascertained by examining the inherent risk and endurance of the company. After proper reflection on the relative performance of the company in terms of Potential and Resilience, the position on the PARE chart can be plotted.

For maximum strategic benefit, it is advantageous to expand the PARE chart to include the specific cause(s) for the firm's falling into a given PARE category. The expanded PARE chart shown in figure 4-1 shows that there are sixteen PARE classes into which the company can be placed: one for PARE I (no problems with any of the strategic elements relative to the reference firm), three for PARE II (Potential problems), three for PARE III (Resilience problems), and nine for PARE IV (difficulties with both Potential and Resilience).

This expanded comparative analysis chart serves a purpose that is more than a matter of cosmetic embellishment. The important distinctions between the two strategic elements that interact to determine each of the Key Strategic Factors enrich the analytical power of the PARE tool of management. By showing that the outward manifestations of problems with Potential or Resilience (or in a conventional analysis in terms of return and risk) may be caused by fundamentally different, predominantly internal deficiencies, more attention is devoted explicitly to the source of the problem. There is great danger with an analysis that ignores this strategic differentiation because reacting to Potential and Resil-

			RESILIENCE PROBLEMS		
		Strong:	Weak		
		No Problems	Mainly Risk	Mainly Endurance	Both Risk & Endurance
Strong:	No Problems	I	IIIa	IIIb	IIIc
POTENTIAL PROBLEMS — Weak	Mainly Opportunities	IIa	IVa	IVb	IVg
	Mainly Action Range	IIb	IVc	IVd	IVh
	Both Opportunities and Action Range	IIc	IVe	IVf	IVi

PARE posture I: the company has neither Potential nor Resilience problems relative to the reference firm and is in a dominant position.

PARE posture II: the company has Potential problems relative to the reference firm, but has no problems with Resilience.

PARE posture III: the company has Resilience problems relative to the reference firm, but has no problems with Potential.

PARE posture IV: the company has problems with both Potential and Resilience relative to the reference firm.

Figure 4-1. PARE or Comparative Analysis Chart (Expanded)

ience (or return and risk) in their aggregated form may be akin to treating outward symptoms rather than root causes. Attacking symptoms rather than the more fundamental underlying deficiencies can lead to an exacerbation of the real problem.

The ramifications of falling into a particular class according to the expanded PARE chart can be radically different for a firm than if it were placed in another class, even if both indicate difficulties with the same strategic factor. For a company with a Resilience problem, eliminating or rejecting high-risk projects can be suboptimal if the reason for the difficulty is rooted in the short-term endurance dimension. Similarly, a firm can have many promising opportunities and yet still have a problem with Potential if it cannot obtain the specialized talent required to exploit the opportunities successfully. It should be obvious that these subtle but important distinctions have to be included in the project set preplanning process. However, the danger of errors of omission is great if they are not included explicitly in the analytical framework in a strategically structured way. With all sixteen PARE classes, the ability to differentiate between often crucial situations that require a very specific set of actions for correction is enhanced.

Identification of the PARE position of the company under analysis relative to the reference firm can be conducted in the above strategically structured manner by typifying the company's current posture. This current position is referred to as the *departure situation.* With the aid of this tailored method, strategically applicable preplanning suggestions for actions can be derived. This approach will minimize the danger of situationally unjustified generalizations.

Defining the departure situation less comprehensively tends to blur or to reduce dimensionally the amount of unambiguous information that can be gleaned from such an analysis. This information is vital for giving clear signals about how the firm can effectively react to the challenges of the environment.

INTERDEPENDENCY ENHANCEMENT OF THE PARE ANALYSIS

It is desirable to enhance further the power of the departure situation analysis in the expanded PARE perspective by referring to the impact or ramifications of actions on the four basic elements (and thus on the two key strategic factors). The impact of an action on a strategic element is said to be direct when there is an unbroken connection or a straight bearing of the action upon such an element. Implied in this is a cause-effect relationship independent of the impact of the action on all other strategic elements. The result of managerial actions is defined as having an indirect impact on a strategic element when there is not a direct linkage between cause and effect; rather the impact results indirectly from changes in another basic element or elements. For example, securing a bank line of credit to back up the outstanding commercial paper of a company can improve the endurance position directly through an increase in the very short-run liquidity, even if the firm has no intention of drawing on the line of credit except in an emergency. The same line of credit can also have an indirect impact on action range since the increased endurance may permit the firm to be more flexible in responding to opportunities and threats and to utilize its capabilities with greater freedom of action.

The direct and indirect impact of actions should be considered in three dimensions. First, the direction of the impact is of fundamental importance in assessing the action or combination of actions that can best alleviate any strategic problems and enhance the relative position of the firm. Direction can be either favorably impacting or unfavorably influencing. Second, the timing of the impact can also have important ramifications. Timing can be reasonably indicated in terms of short-run, intermediate, and long-range impacts. Magnitude of the impact is the third important dimension. Strong, moderate, or weak impacts can be assessed by managerial estimation, based on judgment and broad industry experience, regarding the signficance of the firm's strategic posture.

It is quite possible that an action taken or contemplated to improve one strategic element can affect from zero to three of the other basic elements. These impacts can be direct for some and indirect for other of these elements at the same time. Also, there may be concurrently both favorable and unfavorable influences on different strategic elements. Both short- and long-run implications of the action in question can also be relevant. In this context, it is conceivable that there are contrary ramifications for the short and long run. Moreover, magnitude of the impact, often the hardest dimension to assess, may have considerable variation over time and from element to element.

This approach to impact evaluation permits and stimulates explicit inclusion of project set interdependencies in the analysis. In this respect, there are at least three important types of interdependencies that specifically deserve consideration in the preplanning process. Statistical dependence is associated with the extent to which the cash flow from a project moves with or is correlated with the cash flow of the other activities under review. This type of interdependence is normally evaluated within the context of financial diversification and is of paramount importance in many current finance models. Economic dependence refers to the phenomenon by which the costs or benefits expected from one undertaking can differ depending on the acceptance or rejection of other projects. This form of interdependency is assumed to be included in defining the relevant cash-flow streams for finance models. The third type of interdependency is of a social nature and is normally ignored in finance models. Important yet more difficult to grasp than the first two forms, social interdependencies refer to the extent to which activities have task complexities and organizational requirements that are similar and promote their reticulation.

Another concept of statistical dependence is associated with the relative movement of returns from a project with returns from the stock market. This CAPM-based notion is of great significance for many financial decisions, but for the present purpose, measurement and estimation problems render it nonoperational. Additionally, systematic risk of the CAPM focuses attention on market reaction to managerial actions while what is needed is concentration on the actions themselves. This requirement can be fulfilled more satisfactorily through an analysis of the movement of project cash flow with that of the other activities under review. Hence, this approach is adopted.

Failure to include or at least to reflect upon these dependency relationships explictly in the analysis means that many of the strategic considerations that interact directly and indirectly to determine the PARE position of the firm have been assumed away. Strategically meaningful recommendations cannot be made consistently if important problems or essential relationships are presumed not to exist. However, most of the planning models ignore some of these interdependencies and thus are basically incomplete for preplanning purposes.

Assessing all three types of interdependencies within the framework of the direct and indirect impact of actions on the PARE posture encourages proper guidance for the preplanning process. This can be promoted effectively by using an adequate situational typification.

TYPIFICATION OF THE DEPARTURE SITUATION

To assist in identifying the applicable PARE position of the company and in assessing the ramifications of mangerial actions and their interdependencies, a typification method can be developed to specify the departure situation. The typification approach utilizes sequential steps for increasing the specificity of the problem situation in question. It includes both quantitative and qualitative factors deemed by management to be of primary importance for indicating strategic strengths and weaknesses.

The primary focus of this typification methodology is on the medium or short term, without, however, losing too much long-run sight. The predominant long-range aspects are directed more toward identification of particularly advantageous types of projects or geographic areas and timely development of relevant capabilities of the firm.

A delicate balance is required to reach a justified compromise between broad preplanning and situation-specific planning. The more typification steps included in this analysis, the greater the level of micro detail that it is feasible to introduce. However, as more and more steps are introduced, the interrelationships become increasingly complex, and the ability of a manager to assimilate and process the information efficiently decreases. Thus, it is important to balance carefully the trade-off between detail and assessability in order to promote a satisfactory typification. Such a typifying method contains enough relevant data about the most salient perspectives of the preplanning process, but not so much that interpretation of the data is hampered by too much extraneous detail.

To structure the firm's departure situation in a way that yields the strategically most useful perspective, certain business groupings or project classification categories are helpful. All activities of the firm can be classified into one or more strategic business units or SBUs.[36] An SBU is defined as the smallest activity for which meaningful strategic decisions can be made and which has enough common traits regarding marketing, technology, and return-risk prospects. The core activity or core SBU is defined from the financial point of view as that activity from which management expects the highest discounted net cash flow, taking into account future capital investments, as well as operating receipts and expenses. All other SBUs are classified as non-core activities.[37]

The following shorthand notation will now be employed: A_c is the core activity or core SBU and, $A_{\not{c}}$ are the noncore activities (aggregate) or the noncore activities subset. By this notation, $A_{c+\not{c}}$ refers to core and noncore SBUs and thus represents the set of all activities of the firm (the current project set).

Current projects refers to activities that are already being exploited (questions regarding continuation, abandonment, and retrenchment, for example, have to be decided taking relevant plans into account), and approved projects with existing commitments but not yet at a stage to be exploited. *Planned projects* are those for which thorough preparation and concrete definition have been undertaken but without commitments and existing only as plans. The final group of projects is *anticipated possibilities;* depending on the circumstances, this not yet formally planned group may need to be taken into consideration.

The activities of a company can also be classified geographically. In this respect, a geographic area is distinguished as a country or a coherent grouping of countries with enough common socioeconomic traits. The *main geographic area* is distinguished as the area pertinent to the activity(ies) under discussion from which management expects to realize the highest present value of the associated cash flow. All other areas pertinent to the same activity(ies) are labeled as *other geographic areas.*[38]

The geographic areas that are related to the core activity are designated by G_c and for the noncore activities $G_{\not{c}}$. Also, the sub-subscripts "main" and "other" refer to main and other geographic areas. The superscript f can be used to designate cash flow (financial). With this notation the following identities can be formed to clarify the above concepts and thus to reduce the chance of confusion:

$$\textit{Cash flow}_{\text{core}} = A^f_c = G^f_c = G^f_{c_{\text{main}}} + G^f_{c_{\text{other}}}$$

$$\textit{Cash flow}_{\text{noncore}} = A^f_{¢} = G^f_{¢} = G^f_{¢_{\text{main}}} + G^f_{¢_{\text{other}}}$$

$$\textit{Cash flow}_{\text{total}} = A^f_c + A^f_{¢} = G^f_c + G^f_{¢} =$$

$$= G^f_{(c+¢)_{\text{main}}} + G^f_{(c+¢)_{\text{other}}}$$

A parallel set of relationships can also be developed for sales instead of cash flow, substituting the superscript s (sales) for f.

Depending on the needs of the problem situation, employing the SBU and geographic classification schemes can result in a multifaceted and meaningful breakdown of the project set into important decision units. This enhances the power of discrimination in the PARE perspective to arrive at insightful conclusions about the strategic position of the firm and its ability to handle opportunities and threats as they tend to appear. Such a breakdown is also important to extract the maximum usefulness from the BIM analysis in promoting a balanced overall set of preplanning suggestions. Other classifications, such as by resource areas or influence areas, are also possible, but for preplanning purposes, these are not generally required at this stage.

Important characteristics of the departure situation must be identified to begin the typification process. These characteristic factors are specified with respect to their ability to cast light on the company's position according to one or more strategic elements relative to the reference firm. A selection of the most salient of these characteristics is utilized as introductory typification steps. These steps, sequentially applied, indicate the applicable PARE class of the company as unambiguously as possible. They can also signal predominant direct-indirect tendencies for possible management action to improve the company's strategic posture under review.

The typification steps selected for inclusion in this book are presented in detail in chapters 5 and 7 and in the glossary. The typification discussed in chapter 5 is intended to reveal in highlights broad or overall characteristics of the firm from which insight into the PARE position in question can be ascertained. These specific steps should not be thought of as having universal applicability for all companies since certain firms or industrial sectors may require different typification steps to extract relevant information. However, they have proved to be useful for a very wide range of corporations that have been evaluated by this typification method.

At times it may be desirable to investigate more closely the details of the firm's departure situation after the broad typification in highlights has been applied. If required by the situation, more detail can be analyzed with the help of a problem-oriented follow-up. Such a follow-up method is presented in chapter 8. It should be stressed that the danger of confusion and misdirected recommendations is high with attempts to go directly to the greater level of detail possible with the problem-oriented follow-up method. Bypassing the broad typification should not be attempted since general insight into the overall PARE position is essential to give effective direction to further analysis.

To simplify the discussion in the text and as an aid to readers, all of the characterization factors utilized to define the various typification steps are presented in the glossary. Names in alphabetical sequence, definitions, reference points, and classification categories are also included in it.

5 SITUATIONAL SPECIFICATION PROCESS

The PARE-based model for linking the effects of managerial actions to product and capital market reactions can be used to give overall strategic guidance for managing a firm's project set. Typification of the departure situation with carefully selected characterization factors is an important preliminary step for imparting sufficient structure to the analysis. These typification steps should be chosen with two purposes in mind to give adequate insight into the strengths and weaknesses, and thus the strategic posture, of the overall firm. First, a set of typification steps should be chosen so that the departure situation can be characterized in such a way that it gives enough information regarding the four strategic elements for determining the PARE position. Only in this manner will adequate guidance be forthcoming. Second, the minimum number of steps that collectively can shed sufficient light on each of these strategic elements should be utilized. The more steps included in this introductory analysis, the greater the chance of confusion from overcomplexity. Since ten is an appealing round number, we wanted to include no more than this number of steps for introductory typification of departure situations presented in various examples. Unfortunately, it proved impossible to do this without sacrificing too much analytical depth. Fourteen typification steps, broken down into five categories to facilitate presentation, are required to gain sufficient strategic insight for an introductory overall approach.

This set of typification steps appears to have an enriched information content for the intended purpose across a wide spectrum of companies and industries. It should not, however, be considered as applicable to all firms in all situations; the business world is too rich in variety to permit such a universal specification. Thus, in applying the methodology to a specific situation, care must be taken to verify the relevancy and suitability of the typification set for the intended purpose.

SPECIFYING THE TYPIFICATION STEPS

The typification process presented in this book will be introduced and explained by using an example firm. However, several points need to be brought out before presenting the steps and kept in mind as the discussion progresses. The characterization factors that, as components, make up the typification steps are explicated in the text when they are introduced. A more comprehensive although concise explanation for all factors can be found in the glossary at the end of the book. For detailed information about definitions of terms, reference points, and classification schemes, the glossary can be consulted. The applicable number of each item will be mentioned in the text. In principle, each typification step might have an influence on all of the four strategic elements, and perhaps more so on some than others. In the discussion that follows, only the primary influences are emphasized, but consequences in the perspective of the other strategic elements will be obvious from the example under analysis.

Market-oriented Category

Market Share/Market Growth. A growing market provides opportunities for investment and, as such, is a most important factor for appraising the strategic element opportunities. The power of the assessment is increased by coupling market growth with market share since the latter has been shown by Profit Impact of Marketing Strategies (PIMS) studies to be the major determinant of profitability in the sample of firms investigated.[39] In fact, the significance of the combined market share/market growth class is such that the Boston Consulting Group (BCG) has adopted this typification as the essence of its assessment technique.[40]

As portrayed in figure 5-1, the entries for the example firm indicate that the core activity has a market growth rate similar to that of the reference industrial sector and a market share similar to that of the relevant competitor. (Further information on these two reference items can be found in the glossary under items 23 and 35 for market growth and market share, respectively.) For the

		Market Share		
		relatively higher	similar	relatively lower
Market Growth	relatively higher		Non-Core SBUs	
	similar		Core SBU	
	relatively lower			

Figure 5-1. Market Share/Market Growth Survey

aggregation of noncore SBUs of the example company, there is a similar market share but a relatively higher market growth rate.

Figure 5-1 differs from the typical BCG market growth/market share application in some respects. Notice that there are three positions instead of two as in the BCG approach. This and the financially oriented distinction between core and noncore SBUs are both more appropriate for the overall typification at hand.[41]

Familiarity with Markets and Technologies. To be able to compete successfully in the marketplace, a company has to have adequate familiarity both with the applicable technology and with the product markets in which it is participating. In fact, this familiarity is a primary determinant of the competitive strengths of the business. Thus, it is included as a typification step that is particularly important for identifying the action range of the company.

In directional policy matrix approaches, the concepts contained in this step are usually embedded in the assessment of the company position. By breaking them out and considering market familiarity (glossary item 36) and technology familiarity (item 54), apart from other things, more strategic guidance is possible from the analysis.

For the example firm, there are mainly familiar markets for all SBUs utilizing ongoing new technology for the most part. The company position according to this perspective is plotted in figure 5-2, a variant of Ansoff's matrix.[42]

Knowledge and Skill-related Distinctions. This typification step deals with both generalized and specific attributes of the firm's competence. The concept of generalized knowledge and skill refers to general managerial, broad organizational

		Market Familiarity		
		familiar	ongoing new	radically new
Technology Familiarity	familiar			
	ongoing new	EXAMPLE FIRM		
	radically new			

Figure 5-2. Familiarity with Markets and Technologies

and financial capabilities, and understanding within the firm under analysis. The specific attributes are associated with both marketing and product qualities abilities. Specific marketing knowledge refers to the extent to which management and staff of the firm possess information concerning the ability to compete successfully in the relevant market for the activity in question. Product qualities knowledge refers to the assessment by management of the extent to which the firm possesses information on the product under study pertinent to how closely the product reflects the qualities required by customers, and any needed changes to meet such requirements better. For both specific components, skill represents the extent to which the company has the ability to exploit the respective knowledge.

Also, there is an important distinction between the knowledge and skill required to accomplish the firm's objectives and that which is available. These concepts are, in principle, contained in directional policy matrix approaches, although clearly not in sufficient detail to differentiate between requirements and availability. Thus they lack the ability to assess the action range of the firm in a manner that is as meaningful as with this typification step.

The position of the example company is shown in figure 5-3. In this example, the availability of general knowledge and skill is relatively greater than the requirements. For marketing-specific knowledge and skill, as well as for product-specific knowledge and skill, the availability is equal to the requirements. Since this is one of the most complex typification steps, verifying each of the included characterization factors by referring to the appropriate items in the glossary is recommended. The availability factors are items 3, 4, 5, 6, and 19; the requirements factors are items 20, 44, 45, 46, and 47.

			REQUIREMENTS FOR GENERAL KNOWLEDGE AND SKILL					
			low			high		
			Marketing Specific Knowledge and Skill			Marketing Specific Knowledge and Skill		
			Required Less Than Available	Required Equal to Available	Required Greater Than Available	Required Less Than Available	Required Equal to Available	Required Greater Than Available
AVAILABLE GENERAL KNOWLEDGE AND SKILL	high	Product-Specific Knowledge and Skill: Required Less Than Available						
		Required Equal to Available		EXAMPLE FIRM				
		Required Greater Than Available						
	low	Product-Specific Knowledge and Skill: Required Less Than Available						
		Required Equal to Available						
		Required Greater Than Available						

Figure 5–3. Knowledge and Skill-related Distinctions

Cash-flow-oriented Category

Cash-flow Margin of the Firm. Cash-flow margin, or the amount of net cash flow generated for each dollar of sales, is a primary determinant of the profitability of the aggregated SBUs and the ability to generate returns for a given amount of investment. Furthermore, the concept of cash-flow margin is important since, from learning curve theory, the lower the unit cost, the better able the firm is to compete in the product market.[43] This implies that the higher the cash-flow margin, ceteris paribus, the more pricing flexibility the company has and thus the more competitive the firm is. The cash-flow margin also gives an indication of possible flexibility that a company may have in channeling funds to other opportunities. For these reasons, cash-flow margin is particularly useful for shedding light on the action range of the firm.

For the example company, the cash-flow margin is assumed to be similar to that of the reference firm. More detail about the specification of this concept can be found in item 7 in the glossary.

Cash-flow Balancing for Future Requirements. Cash-flow balancing for future requirements is a particularly meaningful combination of characterization factors that introduces the time dimension into the analysis. The role of this typification step is to evaluate the extent to which the internally generated cash flow, supplemented by external capital acquisitions, is balanced between the short and long run. Thus it is quite helpful for evaluating the ongoing action range of the firm, and it also provides information about future opportunities.

As revealed in figure 5-4, cash-flow balancing for future requirements is composed of two characterization factors that work together synergistically. The release of net cash flow in time by the asset investments of the company (glossary item 43) refers to the intertemporal funds generation or the cash requirements pattern of the firm. Funding capacity for financing (glossary item 18) deals with the ability of the company to generate new incremental capital from all sources, both internal and external. By combining these two factors into a single typification step, insight is deepened into the continuing ability of the firm to finance opportunities as they tend to arise.

This dimension of analysis is in harmony with the suggestions by Lorange to include cash-flow timing characteristics in a measure that he refers to as "consolidation attractiveness."[44] Also, the cash-flow implications of falling into the BCG market share/market growth classes can be partially captured here. The example firm has good long-term cash release with a low short-term cash release. Furthermore, the funding capacity for financing is similar to that of the reference firm.

		Funding Capacity for Financing		
		relatively higher	similar	relatively lower
Release of Net Cash flow in Time	primary short-term cash release, low long-term cash release			
	high short-term cash release, good long-term cash release			
	low short-term cash release, good long-term cash release		EXAMPLE FIRM	
	low-short-term cash requirements, primary long-term cash release			
	high short-term cash requirements, primary long-term cash release			

Figure 5–4. Cash-flow Balancing for Future Requirements

Cash-flow/Market-oriented Category

Cash-flow Growth/Sales Growth. Cash-flow and sales growth rates are combined into the representation of a single typfication step (for specification details of the cash-flow growth rate, see glossary item 21 and for sales growth rate, item 25). This typification step is helpful to distinguish the competitive position of the company in the product markets. Further, important information about the cost structure of the firm and its aggregate life-cycle stage can be inferred from this step. Therefore it is most useful for identifying both the opportunities and the action range of the firm.

The cash-flow ramifications of falling into one of the BCG market share/market growth classes is partially covered by this step (other impacts being captured by cash-flow balancing). Additional dynamic information is also provided that is not possible to extract from the usual portfolio techniques. This will become apparent later on during the analysis phase.

As portrayed in figure 5-5, the core SBU of the example firm has relatively higher growth in both sales and cash flow than the appropriately defined reference industrial sector. However, for the aggregation of the noncore SBUs of this firm, there is a relatively higher sales growth but a cash-flow growth that is only similar to that of the reference item.

Concentration of Cash Flow/Concentration of Sales. Concentration refers to the extent to which the cash flow or the sales of the firm come from the core SBU. By combining the two concentration concepts into one typification step, it is possible to gain insight into the balance of the company's activities with respect to profitability and, to some extent, the life-cycle implications. For instance, if sales are more concentrated than cash flow, there is an indication that

		Growth Rate of Cash flow		
		relatively higher	similar	relatively lower
Growth Rate of Sales	relatively higher	CORE SBU		
	similar	NON-CORE SBUs		
	relatively lower			

Figure 5-5. Cash-flow Growth/Sales Growth

the core activity is not as profitable or does not contribute as much to the cash-flow margin as some of the noncore SBUs. Perhaps too much attention is then devoted to the core activity since it may be in a declining phase of the life cycle.

At first glance, it may appear that there is a high correlation between sales concentration and market share, but this is not necessarily so. If two companies are of different sizes and each has the same share of a given market, it may represent 99 percent of the business activity of the smaller firm but only 1 percent of the activity of the larger. Hence, a measure of market share is inadequate to convey the concept of concentration in the most meaningful way.

Such information is not included in most portfolio techniques for strategic evaluation. This is a serious omission since concentration is particularly useful for assessing the risk of the company, although there may also be important ramifications for endurance and action range.

The concentration of cash flow/concentration of sales classification is shown in figure 5-6 (for specifics, including class definitions, regarding cash-flow concentration, see glossary item 9, and for concentration of sales, item 10). For the example firm, both the cash flow and the sales of the core SBU in question are "concentrated".

Environment-oriented Category

Economic Circumstances of Project Areas. Economic circumstances of project areas introduces a geographic dimension into the analysis through the specification of management's perception of the overall economic climate in the geographic areas under study (for more specifics, see glossary item 13). Economic circumstances may, to a limited extent, be included in the measures of business attractiveness utilized in some current portfolio analysis techniques, but only tangentially because they do not consider explicitly the geographic dimension in its financial context.

The evaluation of both the opportunities and the risk faced by the company is facilitated by this typification step. From figure 5-7, it is apparent that the general economic conditions in the main geographic areas of the example firm are predominantly unfavorable. In its other geographic areas, the economic circumstances are mainly good.

Environmental Change Impact. Environmental change impact is another geographically oriented typification step that extends the information content of the economic circumstances of project set areas by reflecting on the likely dynamics into the future. It does this by specifying the manager's perception about the stability or instability of the environment in terms of both the direc-

		Cash flow Concentration of the Core SBU		
		"concentrated"	"dominant"	"dispersed"
Sales Concentration of the Core SBU	"concentrated"	EXAMPLE FIRM		
	"dominant"			
	"dispersed"			
	"diffused"			

Figure 5-6. Concentration of Cash Flow/Concentration of Sales

		Economic Conditions in the "Main" Geographic Areas		
		mainly favorable	mainly good	mainly unfavorable
Economic Conditions in "Other" Geographic Areas	mainly favorable			
	mainly good			EXAMPLE FIRM
	mainly unfavorable			

Figure 5-7. Economic Circumstances of Project Areas

tion and magnitude of the expected change (for specifics on environmental change regarding project return, refer to glossary item 16).

This typification step permits in particular the explicit consideration of the risk faced by the firm in question. At the same time, it is also useful for facilitating the evaluation of the company's opportunities.

Pethia and Saïas advocate the inclusion of a variable for environmental instability in the analysis of the project set.[45] However, they do not differentiate the direction of the change, only the magnitude of the change or degree of instability. This omission detracts from the ability of their analytical technique to yield properly directed guidance for the purpose under study.

It is clear from studying figure 5-8 that the environmental change impact is restricted to the main geographic areas for both the core SBU and the aggregation of the noncore SBUs. For the example firm, there is no appreciable change expected in the main geographic area of the core SBU, but predominantly a small favorable change is indicated in the main geographic areas of the noncore SBUs.

Inflation Impact on Profitability. In the present business climate, inflation is generally conceded to be a very serious problem worldwide. The inflation rate may differ substantially, however, in diverse geographic areas. By including inflation impact on profitability as a typification step, it is possible to permit explicit consideration of the degree of inflation expected by management and the impact of inflation on both the cost and the revenue streams. Inflation impact on profitability thus combines three important characterization factors into one significant typification step.[46] The interaction of inflation sensitivity of project's business cost (glossary item 28) and inflation sensitivity of project's revenue (item 29) reveals the possible impact of inflation on the cash-flow

		Environmental Change in the Main Geographic Area of the Core SBU				
		highly favorable	small favorable	none appreciable	small unfavorable	highly unfavorable
Environmental Change in the Main Geographic Areas of the Non-Core SBUs	mainly highly favorable					
	mainly small favorable			EXAMPLE FIRM		
	mainly none appreciable					
	mainly small unfavorable					
	mainly highly unfavorable					

Figure 5-8. Environmental Change Impact

margin and other net cash-flow-related factors. When combined with the expected inflation degree in the geographic area under analysis (glossary item 27), much relevant information can be extracted.

This typification step is primarily helpful in assessing the risk position of the firm, although it can also cast light on endurance and action range and sometimes on opportunities. The information included in this step is not utilized by any of the popular management techniques except, perhaps, when embedded in an aggregated concept. For instance, a concept such as "shape of cash flow" may be thought of as containing some information about the inflation impact on profitability, but not in the most desirable or useful form.

For the example firm, figure 5-9 shows that inflation in all geographic areas in which this company is active is mainly relatively higher than in the reference country. Also, the greatest impact of this inflation is predominantly on costs rather than on revenues.

Profit/Risk-oriented Category

Operating Profitability/Operating Risk. The operating profitability, defined as the number of present value equivalent dollars of cash inflow for every dollar of capital expenditure, and the operating risk, measured as relative variability of estimated earnings before interest and taxes, are combined in this typification step (for specification of both characterization factors, see glossary items 40 and 49, respectively). This step consists of a reticulated return/risk classification by which the company can be compared to the reference firm. It is particularly useful for assessing both the risk and the opportunities of the company.

		Inflation Sensitivity of Costs and Revenues		
		more impact on revenues than on costs	similar impact on both costs and revenues	more impact on costs than on revenues
Degree of Inflation in Geographic Areas	mainly relatively higher			EXAMPLE FIRM
	mainly similar			
	mainly relatively lower			

Figure 5-9. Inflation Impact on Profitability

		Operating Risk of the Firm		
		relatively lower	similar	relatively higher
Operating Profitability of the Firm	relatively higher			
	similar			EXAMPLE FIRM
	relatively lower			

Figure 5-10. Operating Profitability/Operating Risk

Since most of the other planning techniques focus primary attention on business segments rather than on the firm as a whole, return and risk in the sense embodied here generally tend to be treated too superficially. In order to overcome this limitation, figure 5-10 presents the return/risk position of the example company. There is a similar return, but risk is relatively higher when compared to the reference firm.

Bankruptcy Chance (Long-term Risk). Risk of bankruptcy, or the continued financial viability of the firm in the long run, is approached by looking at the interaction of several important financial variables. The degree of operating leverage (glossary item 31) reveals the sensitivity of operating income to changes in sales. Sales variability (item 59), together with the leverage concept, is a tool for assessing the expected distribution of operating income. Fixed charge coverage (item 17) shows how much variation in operating income the firm can tolerate before it feels financial stress. Thus, this typification step is of primary importance for identifying the risk position of the company, although there are also implications for endurance.[47]

This approach to risk is usually ignored or dealt with inadequately by the various other planning techniques. Their use may have serious consequences because risk is a fundamental determinant of the health of a company. Thus, this typification step refers to an important overall trait that should be considered to make the analysis strategically more useful. For the example company, as revealed in figure 5-11, the fixed charge coverage is relatively lower, the operating leverage is similar, and there is a relatively higher sales variability than that of the reference firm.

Insolvency Chance (Short-term Risk). Even very profitable firms with excellent long-term prospects can get into situations of financial stress in the short run. Risk of insolvency addresses this dimension by considering the interaction of the

		Degree of Operating Leverage								
		relatively lower			similar			relatively higher		
		Sales Variability			Sales Variability			Sales Variability		
		relatively lower	similar	relatively higher	relatively lower	similar	relatively higher	relatively lower	similar	relatively higher
Fixed Charge Coverage	relatively higher									
	similar									
	relatively lower						EXAMPLE FIRM			

Figure 5-11. Bankruptcy Chance (Long-term Risk)

debt maturity structure, or the proportion of liabilities that are short term, with variability of cash flow and the liquidity of the firm (for specific information on these components, see glossary items 11, 56, and 34, respectively).[48] Debt maturity structure reveals the extent of liabilities that are subject to risk from short-run imbalances in cash inflows and outflows, and cash-flow variability shows how volatile they may be. The liquidity of a company indicates how much capital it has in reserve to augment the cash flow, if necessary, to meet short-term obligations as they become due. In addition to the obvious ramifications in the risk perspective, this typification step is one of the more important for assessing the endurance of the firm.

The position of the example company is given in figure 5-12. Coupled with relatively lower liquidity than the reference firm is relatively higher cash-flow variability and a greater proportion of short-term obligations in the financial structure.

Weathering Ability of the Firm. While insolvency risk is concerned with the debt portion of the capital structure, weathering ability focuses on the common stockholders. It deals with the ability of the company to continue paying at least a constant dividend when faced with adversity. Thus, it has ramifications especially for the endurance of the firm, although it can also cast light on the risk side.

Dividends are paid out of the after-tax earnings of a company. To judge the relative volatility of net income, the interaction of sales variability and total leverage of the firm are presented (for specifics on these components, refer to glossary items 59 and 33, respectively). To make the comparison more meaningful, the dividend coverage (item 12), or the amount of net income for each dollar of dividends expected by the market to be paid, is included in this typification step.[49]

This concept is either ignored or undervalued by other planning techniques since they usually are not sufficiently concerned with the impact of actions on the overall firm. Also, they tend to focus not enough attention on the Resilience side of the analysis.

Figure 5-13 shows the position of the example company. Although the total leverage is similar to that of the reference firm, sales volatility of the example company is relatively higher and there is a relatively lower dividend coverage.

RECAP OF THE TYPIFICATION STEPS

The typification steps in these five categories are sufficient to describe adequately with an overall orientation, the departure situation of the firm in diverse perspectives. The steps are balanced with respect to the four strategic elements;

	D E B T				M A T U R		
	relatively lower short-term						
	CASH FLOW VARIABILITY					CASH FLOW	
	very low	relatively lower	similar	relatively higher	very high	very low	relatively lower
LIQUIDITY relatively higher							
LIQUIDITY similar							
LIQUIDITY relatively lower							

Figure 5-12. Insolvency Chance (Short-term Risk)

thus a comprehensive analysis is possible that is compatible with the required variety. This represents a sound approach to introductory identification.

The most salient features of existing techniques are embodied in the steps. Additionally important geographic distinctions are included and information is presented with respect to the long-term and short-run balance of the company. Removing any one of the fourteen steps would disrupt this careful balance and lead to a gap in the coverage of the most important strategic dimensions of pre-planning. A summary of the typification steps for the example firm follows to facilitate a surveying of its main characteristics (this recap is important since this firm will play a central role in the next chapters).

A. Market-oriented Category

1. Market share: Core: similar; noncore: similar
   Market growth: Core: similar; noncore: relatively higher
2. Familiarity: Markets: familiar; technology: ongoing new
3. Knowledge and skill: Generalized: availability greater than required; specific: balanced

B. Cash-flow-oriented Category

4. Cash-flow margin: Similar
5. Cash-flow Balancing: Good long-term cash release, low short-term cash release; similar funding capacity for financing

I T Y			S T R U C T U R E				
similar			relatively higher short-term				
VARIABILITY			CASH FLOW VARIABILITY				
similar	relatively higher	very high	very low	relatively lower	similar	relatively higher	very high
						EXAMPLE FIRM	

C. Cash Flow/Market-oriented Category

6. Cash-flow growth: Core: relatively higher; noncore: similar
   Sales Growth: Core: relatively higher; noncore: relatively higher
7. Concentration of: Cash flow: concentrated; sales: concentrated

D. Environment-oriented Category

8. Economic circumstances: Main areas: mostly unfavorable; other areas: mainly good
9. Environmental change: Main areas of core: none appreciable; main areas of noncore: mainly small favorable
10. Inflation impact on profitability: Relatively higher inflation, greater impact on costs than revenues

E. Profit/Risk-oriented Category

11. Operating profitability: similar; Operating risk: relatively higher
12. Bankruptcy chance: Fixed charge coverage: relatively lower; operating leverage: similar; sales variability: relatively higher
13. Insolvency chance: Debt maturity structure: relatively higher; short-term liquidity: relatively lower; cash-flow variability: relatively higher
14. Weathering ability: Dividend coverage: relatively lower; total leverage: similar; sales variability: relatively higher

		TOTAL LEVERAGE OF THE FIRM								
		relatively lower			similar			relatively higher		
		SALES VARIABILITY			SALES VARIABILITY			SALES VARIABILITY		
		relatively lower	similar	relatively higher	relatively lower	similar	relatively higher	relatively lower	similar	relatively higher
DIVIDEND COVERAGE	relatively higher									
	similar									
	relatively lower						EXAMPLE FIRM			

Figure 5-13. A Company's Weathering Ability

6 DERIVING BALANCED RECOMMENDATIONS FOR ACTION

Reflecting back on the development of strategic analysis, it will be clear that the effective and efficient allocation of corporate resources demands reflection on many alternatives and various considerations. In what some would argue is a too variety-rich environment, analytical tools must be developed to filter out the irrelevant information, structure the data, and draw from them justified implications and recommendations. Two methods have been described that are of help in filtering and structuring information effectively: the typological approach to problems and the PARE method. In this chapter these concepts are operationalized more concretely through a step-by-step examination of the departure situation developed in chapter 5 for the example firm. This process leads to typification-based recommendations. Furthermore, attention is paid to an analytical method that lessens the chance of errors of strategic omission and promotes well-proportioned balancing of the trade-offs between contrasting considerations. In this respect, it is helpful to examine the recommendations derived from the typification—as an additional check—in the perspective of the Balancing Identification Method (BIM).[50] After an in-depth explanation of BIM and how it can be used to achieve more efficient action plans, the PARE-based recommendations for strategic improvement regarding the example firm are reviewed.

ANALYSIS OF THE DEPARTURE SITUATION

Now that the departure situation of the example firm has been structured by the fourteen typification steps, the PARE position can be determined rather easily. In fact, the visual presentation of figures 5-1 through 5-13 would probably already lead to an impressionistic PARE positioning when it is realized that the upper left-hand corner of each chart tends to be the most favorable position. However, systematic investigation of the typification steps in terms of each of the strategic elements will provide greater insight into the dynamics of the situation. By doing so, there will also be less of a chance that important information might be overlooked. Thus, opportunities and then action range are evaluated in determining the Potential position of the example firm. Further, risk and endurance are examined and the Resilience position ascertained. This reflection will reveal the applicable PARE class for the example company.

Opportunities

The fact that there is a good long-term cash release from current projects indicates that the aggregated activities are rewarding for the long run. The capital market perception appears to be that the firm's return prospects are rather good. This conclusion stems from the fact that external financing is available to augment the low short-term cash release so that the funding capacity for financing is similar to that of the reference firm.

Both the core SBU and the noncore activities have market shares that are mainly similar to those for the relevant competitors. Also, for the core activity, the market growth rate is similar to that of the reference industrial sector. The noncore activities have market growth rates that are mainly higher than the median sector. Thus, it appears that at least some of the noncore SBUs are in higher-growth, earlier life-cycle stages than the core SBU is. This tends to reinforce the idea that the firm has good future opportunities.

The example firm is possibly more aggressive than the competition, as reflected in relatively higher sales-growth rates for all activities. There may be some reason for concern, however, since the noncore SBUs have cash-flow growth rates that are mainly similar to those of the relevant competitors. This could be the result of price cutting to gain market share, but it should be watched to ensure that it does not lead to future problems. The core SBU does not seem to be experiencing this problem since the cash-flow growth rate is also higher than that of the relevant competitors.

There is a similar operating return (but a relatively higher operating risk) when compared to the reference firm. If pricing cutting to gain market share is occurring in the noncore SBUs, this may explain why the operating return is only similar. This point should be investigated further to determine whether a more serious problem is causing a return/risk imbalance.

One area of possible concern is that both sales and cash flows are relatively concentrated in the core activity while at the same time the general economic circumstances are mostly unfavorable in the main geographic areas. All other opportunities signals are positive or only slightly mixed, so it appears that the example firm may need to pay more attention to some of the better noncore SBUs, predominantly in the other geographic areas where the economic circumstances are mainly good.

This analysis indicates that the company has rather attractive opportunities. There is some cause for concern that further price cutting to gain market share might lead to future problems with cash-flow margin, but if treated with enough caution, it is not a serious item. Regarding the problem of more immediate concern—the concentration of effort in areas with generally unfavorable economic circumstances—feasible opportunities have been identified to overcome any possible difficulty.

Action Range

From the financial point of view, the funding capacity for financing and the cash-flow margin are both similar to those of the reference firm, thus indicating that the action range is satisfactory. The example company is operating in areas with relatively higher than average degrees of inflation, so the greater sensitivity to inflation of costs than revenues will tend to squeeze the cash-flow margin. Perhaps this may be another explanation for the difference between sales and cash-flow growth rates for the noncore SBUs. If so, some action should be taken, such as ensuring that proper opportunities are exploited and costs are reduced as much as possible, to prevent a deterioration of the currently favorable action range. Given the good opportunities and capabilities available to the firm, this should prove not too difficult to accomplish.

The excess availability of generalized knowledge and skill over requirements indicates good action range from a nonfinancial point of view. This is lent further support by the fact that there is sufficient specific product and marketing knowledge and skill to meet requirements. Also, the example firm is operating in familiar markets with ongoing new technology. It is evident that this firm has an adequate action range. Thus, the above analysis of opportunities and action range permits the conclusion that the Potential of the company under study is quite strong.

Risk

The risk of bankruptcy for the example firm is higher than for the reference firm even though they have similar operating leverage. This situation transpires as a result of the relatively higher sales variability coupled with a relatively lower fixed-charge coverage. Since the total leverage is also similar, the implication is that financial leverage is also roughly the same. Perhaps the lower fixed-charge coverage is brought about by a greater use of leasing.

Geographically there is a problem with the economic circumstances in the main geographic areas of all SBUs, but for the noncore activities, conditions are improving. The higher sales variability, in connection with the similar operating leverage, has resulted in a relatively higher level of operating risk for the company than for the reference firm. Furthermore, the inflation-induced question might cause the risk position to deteriorate.

From these considerations, it appears that the example firm has a risk problem. The main causes appear to be the relatively higher sales variability and the poor economic circumstances in the main geographic areas. Other difficulties, such as the lower fixed-charge coverage and the inflation-induced tendency to degrade the cash-flow margin, also need to be reflected upon, but they are of a lesser magnitude.

Endurance

From the perspective of endurance, there are several troublesome tendencies. The relatively lower fixed-charge coverage associated with the relatively higher bankruptcy chance is indicative of a higher-than-average proportion of fixed charges. Much of the debt financing appears to be short term. Considered with the relatively higher cash-flow variability and lower liquidity position, it appears that there is a much greater chance of short-term financial stress for the example company than for the reference firm.

The weathering ability of this company is also less than for the reference firm. Perhaps a partial clue to the company's difficulties is contained in the relatively lower times-dividends-earned. If the company's payout ratio is higher than that of the reference firm, a number of problems with endurance, risk, and action range would be aggravated still more. If cutting the cash dividend were feasible (or holding it constant to decrease the payout ratio over time), less short-term borrowing would be required at high fixed cost, more liquidity would be possible, and fixed charges could be reduced.

Another indication of relevance to the endurance position is the concentration of both sales and cash flow coupled with the mainly unfavorable general economic circumstances in the main geographic areas. The more concentrated are sales and cash flow, the greater the risk, but there is also the danger of a further deterioration of the endurance position. Major strikes or other disruptive actions could interrupt the bulk of the cash inflow, with serious short-term endurance ramifications.

It is clear that perhaps the greatest troubles experienced by the example firm are in the area of endurance. All of the important endurance indicators are lower than for the reference firm, and there are signs of continuing deterioration.

Given difficulties with risk and particularly with endurance, the Resilience of the company must be classified as relatively weak from both perspectives. A further erosion can be expected if management does not take timely steps to reduce costs, eliminate projects not earning enough return to compensate for the risk, and shift the emphasis of the firm geographically to more promising areas. Thus, the conclusion is that, in terms of the expanded PARE chart in figure 3-1, the example firm is in PARE position IIIc because of problems with both risk and endurance.

TYPIFICATION-BASED RECOMMENDATIONS

As a result of the analysis based on the situational typification method, the PARE position of the example firm has been determined and the strengths and weaknesses relative to the relevant reference item have been identified. Now recommendations for action can be investigated.

Even though there is a degree of operating leverage (and total leverage) similar to that of the reference firm, a relatively higher sales variability translates into a greater cash-flow volatility and a higher operating risk for the firm. The impact is exacerbated somewhat by the erosion of the cash-flow margin by both a higher rate of sales growth than that of cash-flow growth and inflation factors. This tends to decrease even further the low short-term cash release by the current activities, necessitating higher short-term borrowing to attempt to maintain an ever-declining liquidity and endurance position. Furthermore both cash flow and sales are concentrated, and the general economic circumstances are unfavorable in the main geographic areas of all projects. These factors lead to the conclusion that the firm has both an endurance and a risk problem that must be resolved. The main emphasis of action plans must be, first, to reduce the cash-flow variability and increase the short-run internal cash generation from existing operations, and then to reduce the geographic risk by a reallocation of effort. There are five action fields for primary concern:

1. Start an intensive cost-reduction program to improve the cash-flow margin and thus the magnitude of cash inflows.

2. Scrutinize during the project set management process, as far as it is compatible with the grand strategy of the firm, the possibilities for accelerating cash inflows and delaying cash outflows.
3. Alter the debt maturity schedule to a more long-term composition.
4. Scrutinize low operating return projects to ensure that the associated risk will be worth the effort.
5. Shift the emphasis for all projects from the main to other geographic areas.

These recommendations, derived from the typified departure situation, are probably an effective combination of actions that can result in an improvement in the strategic position of the example firm. However, the strategic completeness and balance, and thus their efficiency, has not yet been ascertained. BIM is a method to accomplish this reflection and checking process.

THE BALANCING IDENTIFICATION METHOD

Even with a powerful descriptive framework like PARE, it is difficult, without additional aid, to translate a strengths and weaknesses analysis into relevant suggestions for reaction to the environment. Although the PARE method involves a rather broad and comprehensive approach, it is primarily intended as a lead-in for structuring the analysis to preserve manageability. Therefore, it should not be expected to provide complete insight into all dimensions of the strategic assessment and design process.

As supplements to the PARE analysis and for enhancing its value as a managerial tool, a range of significant viewpoints can be identified that repeatedly deserve attention in the exploration for the appropriate strategy. Particular attention should be paid to the purposeful arrangement of these policy considerations in order to achieve a well-balanced strategy.

Such an arrangement can be materialized effectively by paying attention to so-called strategic perspectives during the decision preparation process. In devising each of these salient perspectives, two vital points of view representing coherent but often contrasting facets of strategic behavior are coupled. From the standpoint of methodology, the facet that merits primary study is placed first in the couplet. The other consideration constitutes the complement or counterpoint to the primary point of view. Approaching a problem situation successively from each of these perspectives tends to enhance the identification of a balanced and applicable strategy.[51] This occurs because the methodical selection and pairwise combination of essential viewpoints promotes a proportioned review of different aspects of the situation to balance long-term desirabilities.

Systematic use of these strategic perspectives in a well-ordered surveying process represents the essence of the Balancing Identification Method (BIM).

After using the PARE approach to perceive in highlights the impact of actions on the most important determinants of the value of the firm, BIM can be employed as a useful follow-up for identifying further implications of the departure situation. By reflecting on the related but sometimes contrasting considerations in strategic perspectives, BIM can efficiently guide the balancing search for combinations of actions that, taken together, meet the basic needs of the situation. This reflection process in such perspectives also presupposes an appraisal of the various considerations against the background of the PARE elements: opportunities, action range, risk, and endurance. Therefore BIM forms a vital complement to the PARE approach. When used in conjunction with situational typification under a doing-nothing-strategically-new assumption, relevant indications for effective action can be discovered that are properly adjusted to each other. Thus BIM can function as a useful aid for establishing an acceptable balance between the recommendations by preventing either one or some of them from being out of proportion to the others.

In the discussion that follows, the most salient perspectives of the Balancing Identification Method are explained.[52] In this respect, examples are used to illustrate that the four strategic elements of the PARE method play a significant role in applying it.

Maintenance – Adaptation

In reacting to an environmental situation, an enterprise can maintain the currently outlined strategy; it can also switch to a new line of conduct, which implies strategic adaptation. Continuation of the main points of present practice – maintenance – may well be purposeful. Quite often, sustaining the existing course of action is to be recommended, even in light of alterations in the outside world. Too many changes in strategy can endanger the external as well as the internal continuity of the firm. The continued existence of the company depends on the confidence that it enjoys with its clients. If the direction of the external behavior is being turned too often, that confidence might be lost. Similarly frequent policy changes may be perceived by employees as whimsical and thus can destroy internal confidence.

Each change contains a piece of demolition of values that have formerly been created. For this reason, changes often require paying a high price and should be made only if the maintenance of current strategy will lead to even greater sacrifices. Thus, there is a methodical preference for directing attention to the issue of maintenance first, with adaptation following in the basic identification approach to the applicable strategy.

In the situational context concerned, systematic reflection on key problems from this strategic perspective will promote an efficient balancing of maintenance-adaptation considerations. Insofar as the one or the other is compatible with attractive opportunities, a proper action range, acceptable risk, and adequate endurance for the firm under analysis, in principle, either the maintenance or the adaptation of facets of the current line of conduct are valid.

The case of a distiller of hard liquors with chemical ancillary activities is an example of a situation in which adequate attention was not paid to the continuation of the existing strategy. In the beginning of the 1960s, opportunities in the expansive chemical industry seemed exciting. Historically the English firm Distillers had specialized in the field of relatively simple chemistry of which whisky formed the main item. This company was ill equipped to do so—it had insufficient action range—but it commenced an ambitious entry into the complicated pharmaceutical chemical industry. The problems that arose during the rapid expansion in this new area were grossly underestimated. Especially with respect to research, product development, and technical service, it encountered many difficulties. Thus the opportunities associated with the temporarily high demand disappeared because of the disadvantages from manufacturing and distribution in a rather unknown but intensely competitive field. Eventually the pharmaceutical production line claimed such an amount of corporate resources that the more profitable main activity—distilling—was jeopardized. Consequently there was a grave threat that the firm's operations were becoming unfavorable in the light of all four PARE elements. As a result, a reformulation of strategy took place: the pharmaceutical subsidiary was divested and the company returned to its former line of conduct, which, with hindsight, appeared to be the correct one.

On the other side of the coin, if circumstances dictate, the company should be willing to make strategic adjustments in due time. A great attachment to historical behavior may prove perilous. Several smaller companies in the English textile industry experienced this kind of danger during the past years. In England, as elsewhere, the shift in demand to synthetic textiles was manifested. Because of this shift, substantial overcapacity, and rapidly growing competition, modernization of production machinery appeared to be necessary much earlier than was expected by the majority of the managers. Many textile firms failed to recognize the shift in opportunities and thus did not change their growth and product strategies in time. For this reason, necessary funds for adequate adaptation of the action range of the firms in question were not forthcoming soon enough. This unwarranted maintenance of inappropriate policies helps to explain why many smaller textile mills were either absorbed by great chemical companies in the field of man-made fibers or went out of business.

Individual Action—Joint Action

No company operates completely isolated from competitors; there are always some mutual interests with other companies. Realizing that there are antitrust implications, firms establish links with other companies, often as casual forms of cooperation. For instance, competitors might execute reciprocally large export orders, or there may be a mutual specialization in different classes of quality. Even the peaceful maintenance of a certain status quo in a market may be a tacit form of coexistence.

Each enterprise, however, will have to preconceive its own characteristics and individual interests and define its line of conduct accordingly. Here again one can speak of coherent though also contrasting or sometimes conflicting viewpoints when exploring the applicable strategy. The issues in the perspective individual action—joint action have to be investigated by reflection, considering the four basic PARE elements, on their impacts with respect to the firm's situationally conditioned goals for improvement. The methodical preference for first concentrating attention on the attributes of the firm by itself before assessing the desirability of joint action with third parties is evident as experience with joint ventures shows. Recently in the United States, many of these ventures, concluded enthusiastically for mutual research, development, or manufacturing new products, have not worked out well in practice. One of the reasons that the initial fervor has waned is that too little attention was paid to latent, long-term conflicts of interest between the partners concerned. The cooperation with respect to many of these ventures was terminated within a period of five years, with great losses. These breakdowns can be traced back to devoting insufficient concentration to the company's distinctive competence—its action range—and the diverging concerns of the parties in the long run.

An exaggerated notion of possible but not probable conflicts also occurs. Fruitful collaborations as a supplement to individual action, which can be valid in numerous situations, are often never born. This clearly happened in some parts of the Dutch textile industry. Repeated exhortations from chambers of commerce in textile areas to cooperate selectively in order to improve manufacturing efficiency did not meet with a wide response. As events progressed, this excessive sense of independence to the detriment of the necessary strengthening of both the action range and the endurance of the firms in question was a superficial illusion. The advancing Euromarket belatedly forced joint action among the companies long after they should have started to cooperate. Several textile mills that persisted in their isolationist attitude finally had to liquidate.

Initiative—Caution

The exercise of initiative demands that energetic actions be taken in due time and place without worrying too much about what others might do. Caution, on the other hand, implies vigilance to limit possible damage. In order to be able to exploit the opportunities, in particular in markets with strong competition, due attention should be given to achieving, preserving, and regaining effective initiative. For this reason, in connection with the exploration of strategy, reflection on initiative should methodically come first, with a cautious approach as a follow-up.

Those that miss the initiative repeatedly will, in the end, land with the stragglers. Excessive caution does not guard against all dangers. On the contrary, it might evoke great risks. By giving the competition too often or for too long a chance to take or to hold the initiative, a firm can be driven into a corner and will be forced to take emergency measures. Such an inexpedient reaction will damage the profitability of the company and most certainly will disrupt its long-term planning. By taking appropriate initiatives, however, the firm not only can react favorably to changes in the environment, it may also pioneer with surprising activities that are particularly important for placing rivals on the defensive. Once the initiative has been lost, it is difficult to regain, especially when severe competition exists. Therefore the security of a company is not being served adequately by concentrating primarily on cautious behavior; instead intelligent initiatives are required.

Such an approach makes competition reasonably endurable. However, caution is also relevant for tempering and upgrading initiatives. This watchfulness will provide the necessary counterbalance to guard against excessive initiatives that may threaten to deteriorate into recklessness. In principle, initiative—caution topics should be examined in light of applicable goals for improving the firm's opportunities, action range, risk, and endurance.

Two examples can illustrate some of the salient issues in this perspective. During the first postwar decade at Montgomery Ward department stores, caution predominated in its "following" policy. In contrast, Sears, Roebuck and Company pursued a strategy of initiative. The expansion of Montgomery Ward during this period fell behind that of Sears because of an excessive liquidity created out of the fear of a possible downturn of economic conditions. Ward paid for this caution in relative market position. The liquidity, created to meet a disaster that never came, continued to accumulate. Meanwhile Sears opened new branches.

Its energetic strategy gained it much ground on its gigantic competitor. The overcautious preference for ample liquidity at Montgomery Ward led, in 1954, to the odd situation of having $690 million of net working capital against a profit of $35 million. Consequently opportunities and action range qualities, such as managerial talent and expertise, had deteriorated substantially.

The opposite case shows that an excess of or inappropriate initiatives can be very damaging. This is strikingly illustrated by the petrochemical industry during the last two decades. In this period, the chemical industry was a model of uncurbed expansion as companies raced to reap profits from the opportunities in their field. In spite of rapidly increasing capacity, investment continued without enough vigilance for the inherent risk. Mishaps were bound to occur. Many of the companies that joined uncritically in the last phase of the run on the market suffered heavy losses and often could not recover their complete investment.

Growth – Harmonization

In this strategic perspective, attention to growth refers to a tendency to exploit the Potential of the company as much as possible. In this respect, the strategic element of opportunities is in the limelight. Harmonization, as a contrasting pendant, means care for a well-proportioned adjustment of the strategy under investigation. This carefulness is useful for reminding that due regard also has to be given to the other PARE elements – action range, risk, and endurance – during the identification process.

Endeavoring to achieve growth normally characterizes a healthy and dynamic enterprise; however, concentration on growth also creates the danger that the firm's project set will lose well-balanced proportions. To follow up the focus on growth, enough diligence with respect to harmonization is essential to avoid long-term disequilibria. Thus, for adequate identification of appropriate guidelines, a study of harmonization is also necessary.

As a rule, growth progresses by fits and starts, and therefore disturbances are inevitable, particularly in the short run. The implications of such disturbances cannot be ignored, but at the same time it must be kept in mind that the promotion of growth is of primary importance for the effective development of the company. Consequently, in this perspective, there is methodical preference for first directing attention to the promotion of growth and then to the consideration of well-proportioned harmonization as a supplement in the strategic assimilation process.

The expansion strategy at Breedbank in the Netherlands, a subsidiary of the international iron and steel firm Hoogovens, demonstrates this well-grounded sequence. From the beginning, primary attention was directed to promoting high growth in a rewarding field. Because of growth, cost, and economies of scale relationships, preference was given to the acquisition of a continuous hot-rolling installation for steel sheets, which had a much larger capacity than and was partially incompatible with the other production equipment in the existing manufacturing line. Before this installation was purchased, however, a supplementary check was made to determine whether initial running-in and break-in phases would be feasible considering satisfactory marketing, personnel, and financial consequences. Thus the exploration of the growth prospects was complemented by an adequate harmonization preview. In spite of temporary disturbances caused by having to increase the capacity of the other equipment in the manufacturing line to be compatible, it appeared that the large rolling machine was optimal. With an eye on the profits that could be realized at a later stage, it was thought desirable to permit production to grow into the substantial excess capacity of the manufacturing process associated with the investment decision under study. After this thorough preparation process, the resulting decision proved to be successful as the market development progressed.

Reflection on a situation characterized by a preoccupation with growth is offered as a contrast. A one-sided emphasis on growth opportunities alone, while neglecting the balance of the operations in the context of the other three PARE elements, could portend disaster. An example of this is the case of the electronics branch of the American Ampex Company, which underwent a rapid postwar growth. This enormous growth, however, concealed a great vulnerability. Sales increased in the 1950s from $1 million to $73 million; profits increased from $0.1 million to $4.0 million, implying that they lagged behind sales growth. The net result was that profit became extremely sensitive to a slight decline in sales. The ramifications of this dramatic increase in operating leverage and the resulting decrease in endurance became evident in the early 1960s when annual sales declined from $73 million to $70 million. This fall in business volume was modest. Yet the profit of $4 million fell to a loss of $3.9 million. The company had lost its flexibility and had to contend with serious management problems. It had grown too fast in a strategically unjustified way.

Concentration—Spread

Concentration refers to a focusing of operations and resources to counteract and overcome in due time and place expected resistance toward planned actions. Spread is related to the dispersion of means and activities over time and over various products and markets. These related but often contrasting viewpoints constitute another strategic perspective for the balancing identification process. Concentration of actions and resources, when and where appropriate, is essential to be able to exploit effectively the opportunities that present themselves. Appropriate identification presumes that attention is paid first to the concentration aspect and afterward to the spread facet in preparing for the choice of the valid strategy.

The spread issue should be examined as a follow-up to reflecting on concentration. If done the other way around—spread and then concentration—there is a great danger that the activities and/or the resources of the company will be scattered to such an extent that it may be very difficult to conquer market resistances anywhere. In the concentration/spread perspective, a further recommendation is to ensure that important tendencies with respect to the strategic elements—the opportunities, the action range, the risk, and the endurance of the company under analysis—are not overlooked.

Examples from practice illustrate these important considerations. In this respect, the technical and commercial development in the field of raw materials for plastics can be cited. Many companies entered in an early phase of evolution of this industrial sector. Some approached matters very ambitiously and aimed their efforts at a complete range of groups of plastics. Others concentrated on one or a few groups of plastics. The development of raw materials such as polyvinyl chloride, polyethylene, polystyrene, and methylacrylate for application to high-pressure molding is an example of the extent of problems that can be encountered. In this particular field, the firms were confronted with difficult and costly research and production, as well as with arduous promotion of sales. Each category of raw materials, in its turn, raises its own specific technical and marketing problems. Given the nature and the extent of these problems, the attractiveness and the feasibility of the firm's opportunities should have been scrutinized reflecting in particular on the actual and latent action range implications with respect to concentration—spread issues.

Companies that spread their forces thinly among the different groups of plastics scored remarkedly few successes. In contrast the companies that practiced a wiser restraint in this strategic perspective and concentrated primarily on only a few groups of raw materials prospered. Especially after successful implementation of their main activities, they paid efficient attention to spread issues.

This illustration does not mean that dangers of excessive concentration do not exist. Some middle-sized American oil companies did not, in an early phase, see commercial advantages to the natural gas that was released with their oil drilling. Other industries preceded them in effecting a successful spread of business by the exploitation of this by-product. Only after saturation of the market in certain areas did these oil companies realize that both rewarding opportunities and a suitable action range were also present in this area. By that time, however, it was too late for some of them to be able to profit on a large scale. Their managers had only been thinking in terms of the limited notion of oil instead of the much larger conception of energy. These managers missed very attractive chances to diversify, even though there were many early and easy to exploit opportunities.

Shifting of Action—Change in Intensity

This strategic couplet of coherent yet sometimes contrasting viewpoints is of the greatest importance when exploring policies under dynamic circumstances. Shifting refers to a diversion of the main emphasis of the activities of a company—the conversion to another center of gravity—as a result of altered conditions. The change of intensity is associated with the tendency to vary the pressure that the company exercises in the market and/or the vigor of its technological activity as a reaction to the actual dynamics. Reflection is needed on applicable considerations in this perspective, bearing in mind any situationally conditioned improvement goal with respect to the four PARE elements, for balancing the strategy under review.

Breaks with the past in terms of the nature of competition, market share, and technological development can force the company to make strategic choices in which both shifting of actions and changing the intensity of efforts play a part. In order to respond appropriately to the emerging situation, it is necessary to reflect on both facets of behavior. This also deserves recommendation considering the challenge in dealing with a limited supply of resources.

The two points of orientation, if looked upon in isolation, have little meaning when searching for an adequate strategy. Methodically it is essential that when managers consider altering the intensity of the firm's efforts, they should also give a close examination to the possible effectiveness of shifting the main emphasis of actions. In practice, this is sometimes overlooked, which in turn may lead to a dangerous one-sidedness.

To illustrate this danger, another example from the European textile market is relevant. Since the Euromarket became operational, the character of the competition in the wool industry has drastically changed. After each reduction of import duties, the Italian competition in woolens was clearly felt more strongly in other areas of the Euromarket. The traditional thread center of Prato became especially important because the wages and social costs in the Italian textile industry were considerably lower than in the other countries in the European Economic Community. Also, the Prato center made greater use of substantial numbers of cheaper homeworkers.

The reaction by other competitors in the emerging common Euromarket varied. Some of the firms decided to implement a gradual but timely changeover from conventional woolen threads to worsted. In this market the operating costs are much more uniform, so the companies that switched in time landed in much healthier competitive conditions. As a consequence of this shift of the main emphasis of the activities, they could also profit from the growing demand for the improved and more lucrative style that made its appearance in the areas of the worsted. Thus, in reacting to their basic problem of Potential, managers of these firms reflected appropriately on the pertinent strategic elements—opportunities and action range—in the proper dynamic way.

Another group of the threatened concerns followed a completely different course. In order to maintain their market position in the Prato genre, they engaged in a price war that saw margins continually fall. Because of their myopic preoccupation with price rivalry in the conventional business sector, for many of these firms this cutthroat competition was fatal. Whereas a shifting of activities in due time was indicated, they limited themselves to intensifying the pressure in the old, well-known market. Their undoing is a typical example of a misconception in the perspective shifting of actions—change in intensity by paying inadequate attention in particular to three of the PARE elements: opportunities, action range, and risk.

Each of the previous six couplets refers to a methodical arrangement of generic aspects that are useful for a balanced identification of the applicable strategy. During this balancing process, successive attention is paid to reflection on the effective interaction between long-term considerations in each of the six BIM fields of view. In this way, the probability of unwarranted fluctuations in strategic management can be decreased. In each of these six perspectives of related and sometimes contrasting viewpoints, BIM again and again promotes awareness of the danger of exaggeration from one or the other outlook. Reflection on the disadvantages resulting from preoccupation with one point of view will inherently focus on the advantages of giving greater scrutiny to the countervailing viewpoint. This approach to a problem under analysis tends either to stimulate or moderate the attention directed to the facet in question that generated—in the first instance—too little or too much interest.

As a recapitulation, figure 6-1 portrays the six BIM perspectives that, in dynamic circumstances, are most salient for a well-proportioned identification of the valid straetgy.[53] This representation demonstrates that exploration of the possibilities for variation, with respect to long-term considerations, is conducted successively from the BIM fields of view, but examination in each of these perspectives forms only part of a wider strategic approach.

BIM is strategically sound only if the pertinent investigation process departs from situationally conditioned recognition of the improvement goals considering the four PARE elements. A combination of PARE and BIM for both the determination of strengths and weaknesses and the development of suggestions

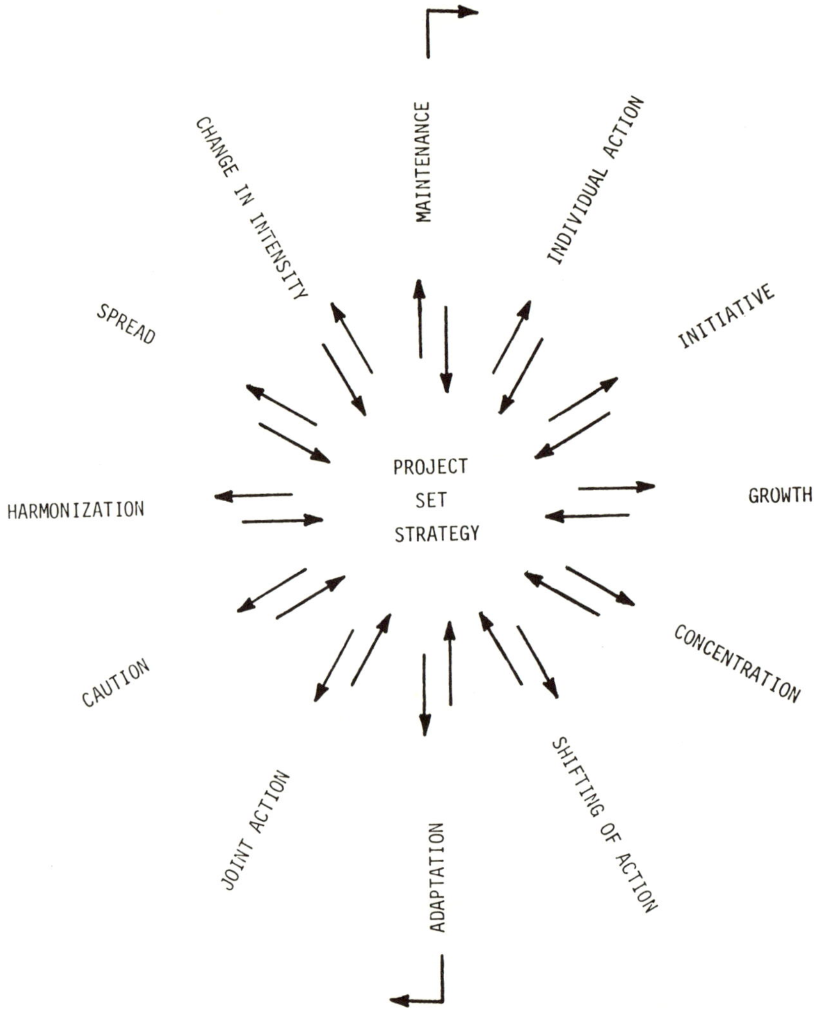

Figure 6-1. Survey of BIM Perspectives

for changes in strategy combines the advantages of both methods synergistically.[54] This synthesis offers guidance on how to adapt strategically, maintaining both structure and balance, to the consequences of complexity and change. By following this guidance, the firm can consistently realize better capital market and product market positions. In this respect, the balance-promoting attributes of BIM are particularly useful for focusing attention on underlying and often implicit assumptions or value judgments of management. This will expose these suppositions for conscious reflection. Therefore, the next section will be devoted to using BIM in the PARE perspective. In this respect, BIM is employed to check for both strategic completeness and proper balance in the typification-based recommendations that appeared earlier in this chapter with respect to the example firm.

BALANCE VERIFICATION WITH THE HELP OF BIM

Maintenance—Adaptation Issues

The policies pursued by the example firm have enabled it to attain a favorable market position with a reasonably good Potential. In this respect, maintaining the main points of the present course of action concerning opportunities will be effective. It is indicative, however, that without corrective action regarding the other component of Potential, current trends will start to have a negative impact on the firm's financial competence in the not-too-distant future. An adjustment is required in the action range strategy to ensure the timely availability of adequate funds for exploiting the most interesting opportunities.

The primary problem areas are on the Resilience side, so a serious question is raised about the appropriateness of the company's present strategy. The guidelines with respect to endurance must be adapted to increase the short-run flexibility of the firm in question. Furthermore, the risk policy has to be changed to reduce risk—both product and geographically associated.

Individual Action—Joint Action Considerations

The example company has a rather strong market position from the opportunities perspective and has a large number of qualities that can be exploited successfully by individual action. This is especially evident in fields in which the firm's competence is very good, such as the core SBU and a few of the noncore activities. The rather serious Resilience problems, however, reduce drastically the flexibility that the firm has in exploiting some of its opportunities successfully. Management needs to consider investigating the possibilities for entering selectively into a joint venture with a financially sound but opportunity-poor company in some of the noncore activities with higher risk. The activities considered should be evaluated particularly in terms of sales variability and high short-term cash requirements. This may improve both the operating risk complexion and the liquidity position, thus mitigating the severity of the Resilience problems now faced by the company under analysis.

Initiative—Caution Issues

It is clear that the good market position that the firm enjoys was obtained by seizing the initiative. But this action has led to an unbalanced behavior that must be reevaluated closely. As a follow-up, a thorough reflection is required for tempering and upgrading initiatives from the perspective of the Resilience problems at hand. Opportunities have to be scrutinized to curtail and refrain further from nonrewarding return projects when considering the associated risk and the company's poor endurance stance. Care is particularly recommended in this respect since insufficient attention has been given to the short-term endurance aspects of the firm's operations. Management has to be prudent to restore a better proportioned balance to the trade-offs between Potential and Resilience considerations. Greater caution is vital in both the short and the long run when exploiting the firm's opportunities in the future. The firm must ensure that the implications for Resilience do not lead to adverse situations in terms of either risk or endurance. Also, particularly for the long term, a deterioration of the currently favorable action range has to be prevented. Bearing in mind the possible erosion of the cash-flow margin by both a higher growth rate for sales than that for cash flows and inflation-induced factors, deterioration is likely. In this respect, care should be taken in approaching opportunities selectively as they emerge.

Growth—Harmonization Considerations

The company has been quite successful in exploiting the growth potential of the markets, but there is an obvious imbalance with respect to harmonization of the strategic proportions. By focusing primarily on the Potential side (and there on opportunities more than on action range) while paying inadequate attention to the Resilience implications, the continuity of a sound growth is threatened. The disturbances resulting from the promotion of growth should be perceived as a signal for a timely adjustment of the course of action. The unfavorable by-effects of preoccupation with the generation and the exploitation of opportunities require enough countervailing vigilance. It is mandatory, therefore, that both the risk and endurance aspects of the corporate strategy be reviewed to harmonize the growth of the firm in the Resilience perspective. In the adaptation process to arrive again at a project set of well-balanced proportions, the care for these aspects has first priority. As a supplementary harmonization, management should take care to avoid a gradual deterioration of the action range in the long run as an effect of future growth. This diligence is relevant since, without an adjustment of the strategy of the example firm, undesirable consequences of endeavors to achieve expansion will result in an unsatisfactory cash-flow margin.

Concentration—Spread Issues

It appears that the firm has been able to concentrate sufficient resources to achieve its market objectives while at the same time spreading out into interesting noncore activities that may have even greater long-run Potential than the core activity. There are, however, problems of risk and endurance in the corporate concentration/spread perspective. To arrive at a more balanced stance, care is advisable to ensure primarily that the distribution of available and latent funds over the firm's opportunities is made with the associated risk and endurance aspects firmly in mind. Therefore it is recommended that in addition to the return assessment, reflection be given to the contribution of investment proposals to both risk reduction and funds generation. In this respect, there is a preference for rewarding projects with a short payback period.

Regarding the product-oriented concentration, it is indicated from both the Potential side and the Resilience perspective that the example firm needs to spread its allocated resources somewhat by paying more attention to some of its better noncore activities. Furthermore, the company's opportunities can be enhanced and corporate risk may be mitigated by changing the present concentration. By devoting incremental efforts to other than the main geographic areas, these benefits can be realized.

Shifting of Action—Change in Intensity Considerations

There is strong evidence that the firm's center of gravity is currently wrong, primarily because of the required adaptation for Resilience reasons, and the latter should be considered as the first priority. Shifting the emphasis for all of the current projects from the main to other geographic areas deserves recommendation. Such shifting is also beneficial for upgrading the opportunities of the example firm. In this respect, some of the most attractive noncore activities will be in the limelight. To be feasible, this shift of actions may require a retrenchment or a risk-sharing arrangement. As a supplement, an applicable adjustment or an adaptation of the intensity of efforts should be considered in the PARE perspective. On the basis of these considerations, the following actions are recommended:

1. Look closely at the noncore activities that have relatively high risk to ensure that their profitability is sufficient to justify their existence. Try to sell off or phase out any projects that are dragging down the firm's operating profitability and to share the risk via a joint venture type of arrangement of particularly risky but sufficiently rewarding projects

(from the point of view of sales variability and short-term cash requirements).

2. Utilize funds freed up in this way to increase the liquidity of the firm and, if sufficient in amount, to shift funds to the best of the noncore activities.
3. Shift the emphasis of the allocation of these funds to the other geographic areas (thus away from the current main geographic areas) to exploit the more favorable general economic situation.
4. Initiate a program to increase the cash-flow margin in light of the relatively higher inflation impact—both by exploiting proper opportunities and reducing costs as much as possible. This step will increase the firm's operating return.
5. Investigate long-term debt consolidation possibilities to change the maturity schedule of the debt.

7 COMPARISON OF TYPOLOGICAL IMPLICATIONS

The recommendations for the example firm derived from the analysis in chapter 6 represent both effective and efficient guidance for action to improve the strategic posture of the company. However, they are very situation specific and cannot safely be generalized to apply to other situations. The reason is that the recommendations are sensitive to the PARE class into which the firm is placed. Different PARE classifications will lead to divergent, sometimes even contrary, suggestions for action. This notion was used to support the argument that the less-comprehensive corporate planning techniques are unable to differentiate adequately between the problem situations represented by the PARE classes and thus can lead to unjustified generalizations in their recommendations. The argument is proved in this chapter.

The ramifications of nonidentical strategic problems are explored to demonstrate the power of the typification-based PARE methodology. Throughout this chapter the example firm will serve as a benchmark for comparing and contrasting changes in departure situations as well as in the resulting recommendations. To facilitate illustration and eliminate confusion, the example firm and its analysis will be designated as the benchmark case.

Attention is focused first on companies with Resilience problems. Since the benchmark case falls within this category, only firms with either mainly risk or mostly endurance problems will be investigated. Both changes in the departure situation and differences in recommendations for these two corporate cases (referred to as the risk case and the endurance case, respectively) are analyzed in light of the benchmark case.

The three PARE classes for companies with Potential problems will then be examined in turn. Each of these classes is compared and contrasted with the benchmark case, the other Resilience cases, and the other two Potential cases to reveal the extent of the differences. It is demonstrated that less-comprehensive corporate planning techniques that cannot distinguish between sometimes subtle but nevertheless strategically important situational characteristics can lead to recommendations that will exacerbate the real problems.

Finally, a PARE I case is discussed: a firm with strong Potential and strong Resilience. From the example cases presented, an appreciation of the analytical depth of the methodology suggested in this book emerges, a depth that cannot be duplicated with any of the other techniques.

No attempt is made in this chapter to explain the detailed reasoning behind the analysis of any of the departure situations. Since the purpose of the chapter is to show the extent of contrasts between recommendations that can arise from the various PARE situational classes, only the differences will be examined in detail. After the in-depth analysis of the benchmark case in chapter 6, the reader will be sufficiently proficient to perform the analysis and derive appropriate suggestions for action.

PROBLEMS FROM THE PERSPECTIVE OF RESILIENCE

PARE position III includes companies that are experiencing Resilience problems of all types. Resilience is composed of the two strategic elements of risk and endurance. Thus the major difficulties could result from endurance deficiencies, unacceptably high risk, or a combination of the two. It is recognized that the concepts of risk and endurance are intertwined and mutually interdependent so as to render at times the isolated consideration of one or the other unrealistic. Nevertheless, it is possible and particularly useful to differentiate between problems that have mainly endurance ramifications or mostly risk implications.

Table 7-1 contains a comparative typification specification for three illustrative cases, all firms with Resilience problems, but which have been placed into nonidentical PARE classes.[55] The first column represents the typification of the benchmark case, analyzed in chapter 6, and is used as the point of departure for discussing the situations for the other PARE classes. To highlight differences between the various cases, any time the classification of an item is the same as for the benchmark case, a dash is inserted in the table. When an entry differs from that of the benchmark case, the classification is specified. For instance, in table 7-1 the fixed-charge coverage for the benchmark case and the endurance case is relatively lower than that of the reference firm, but the risk case has a similar fixed-charge coverage.

Comparing column 2 (risk case) with column 1 (benchmark case) of table 7-1, the differences are primarily of an overall financial nature. There is less chance of bankruptcy or insolvency in the risk case, as compared with the benchmark case, and the weathering ability is stronger. Also, since inflation has similar impacts on both costs and revenues, there is no tendency for the cash-flow margin to deteriorate because of inflation. Thus, in overall financial terms, the firm in the risk case is stronger than in the benchmark case.

These financial characteristics are associated particularly with the firm as an entity and thus cannot easily be identified with particular SBUs or geographic areas. However, this does not imply that the contribution by projects and/or geographic areas to the overall firm characteristics cannot be pinpointed. From these two observations comes a subtle but important distinction between risk and endurance. Endurance tends to be associated with broad, overall firm characteristics and, to a great extent, is of a nature that is most often classified as financial stress situations. Risk can also be associated with overall firm characteristics, but it can also be identified as primarily applying to specific activities in all or in particular geographic areas. With these distinctions in mind, it is clear that the company typified in column 2 of table 7-1 has a stronger endurance position, though a similar risk position, than in the benchmark case.

The situation described in column 3, the endurance case, referring to a firm with mainly endurance problems, is less clear-cut. The differences between it and the benchmark case, however, should still be evident. The alterations in the top three groups of typification steps tend to strengthen—or, at least, not to weaken—the Potential in the endurance case. In the lower two groups of steps, the differences tend to improve both the risk and the endurance perspectives. In contrast to the benchmark case, the main geographic areas of the firm's activities for the endurance case are to be preferred over the other geographic areas in terms of economic circumstances. Both sales and cash-flow variability are lessened so that the operating risk is mitigated. The financial relationships that are of significance for endurance are not as bad, but there are still problems with fixed-charge coverage, debt maturity structure, liquidity, and dividend coverage. Thus endurance remains a problem.

Careful reflection on the factors that caused the PARE classification to change in these three example cases is particularly enlightening. With the possible exception of sales and cash-flow variability, none of these factors are in-

Table 7-1. Typifying Specifications for Firms with Resilence Problems

		Typification Steps		*PARE IIIc: Problems with Risk and Endurance*	*PARE IIIa: Problems Mainly with Risk*	*PARE IIIb: Problems Mainly with Endurance*
A.	1.	Market share	Core	Similar	–	–
			Noncore	Similar	–	–
		Market growth	Core	Similar	–	Rel. higher
			Noncore	Rel. higher	–	–
	2.	Familiarity	Markets	Familiar	–	–
			technology	Ongoing new	–	–
	3.	Knowledge and skill	Generalized	More than needed	–	Balanced
			Specific marketing	Balanced	–	–
			Specific product qualities	Balanced	–	–
B.	4.	Cash-flow margin		Similar	–	–
	5.	Cash-flow balancing	Long-term cash release	Good	–	Primary
			Short-term cash release	Low	–	Low requirement
			Capacity for financing	Similar	–	–
C.	6.	Cash-flow growth	Core	Rel. higher	–	Similar
			Noncore	Similar	–	–
		Sales growth	Core	Rel. higher	–	–
			Noncore	Rel. higher	–	–
	7.	Concentration	Cash flow	Concentrated	–	–
			Sales	Concentrated	–	Dominant

D.	8.	Economic circumstances	Main areas	Unfavorable	–	Good
			Other areas	Good	–	Unfavorable
	9.	Environmental change	Main area of core	None	–	Small favorable
			Main areas of noncore	Small favorable	–	–
	10.	Inflation impact on profitability	Inflation rate	Rel. higher	–	Similar
			Impact on cash flow	Greater on costs	Similar	Greater on revenues
E.	11.	Operating profitability		Similar	–	–
		Operating risk		Rel. higher	–	Similar
	12.	Bankruptcy chance	Fixed-charge coverage	Rel. lower	Similar	–
			Operating leverage	Similar	Rel. higher	–
			Sales variability	Rel. higher	Similar	Similar
	13.	Insolvency chance	Debt maturity structure	More short term	Similar	–
			Liquidity	Rel. lower	Similar	–
			Cash-flow variability	Rel. higher	–	Similar
	14.	Weathering ability	Dividend coverage	Rel. lower	Similar	–
			Total leverage	Similar	Rel. higher	–
			Sales variability	Rel. higher	Similar	Similar

Note: A dash signifies that the classification is the same as for the benchmark case.

Table 7-2. Recommendations for Example Resilience Problems

Recommendations	*PARE IIIc: Endurance and Risk Problems*	*PARE IIIa: Mainly Risk Problems*	*PARE IIIb: Mainly Endurance Problems*
POTENTIAL			
OPPORTUNITIES-RELATED RECOMMENDATIONS			
1. Increase efforts to generate high-growth opportunities			
2. Acquisition or merger to increase the opportunities			
3. Joint venture to increase the opportunities			
4. Increase marketing efforts to open new markets	*	*	
5. Shift allocation of funds to innovation projects			
6. Change the firm's center of gravity			
7. Change the intensity of the firm's efforts			
8. Concentrate resources in the most profitable areas			**
9. Exploit opportunities individually			*
ACTION RANGE-RELATED RECOMMENDATIONS			
1. Shift action range strategy to increase short-term cash available	*		*
2. Accelerate the cash inflow of the core SBU			*
3. Accelerate the cash inflows of the noncore SBUs	*		*
4. Shift funds to high short-term cash release SBUs			*
5. Initiate a cost-reduction program	*		*
6. Buy needed knowledge, skill, and technology			
7. Acquisition or merger to acquire needed knowledge, skill, and technology			
8. Joint venture to acquire needed knowledge, skill, and technology			
RESILIENCE			
RISK-ORIENTED RECOMMENDATIONS			
1. Abandon or sell high-risk projects	**	**	

Table 7-2. continued

Recommendations	*PARE IIIc: Endurance and Risk Problems*	*PARE IIIa: Mainly Risk Problems*	*PARE IIIb: Mainly Endurance Problems*
2. Joint venture high-risk projects to spread the risk	**	*	
3. Exercise more caution in exploiting growth opportunities	*	*	**
4. Revise the operating leverage characteristics of the firm		*	
5. Change the firm's center of gravity to reduce risk	*	*	
6. Shift allocation of funds to lower-risk SBUs	**	**	
7. Shift allocation of funds from higher-risk SBUs	**	**	
8. Shift funds to SBUs with lower cash-flow variability	**	**	
9. Shift funds to SBUs with lower sales variability	**		
ENDURANCE-ORIENTED RECOMMENDATIONS			
1. Increase the short-term flexibility of the endurance strategy	**		**
2. Shift funds to high short-term cash release SBUs	*		**
3. Institute a cost-reduction program	**		**
4. Change the center of gravity for endurance	*		*
5. Revise the debt maturity structure	**		**
6. Revise the debt-equity mix		*	*
7. Exercise more caution in exploiting opportunities	**		*
8. Slow the exploitation of growth until better harmonization with endurance is achieved	**		**

*This suggestion is viable and deserves consideration.

**This recommendation is very important and/or urgent and this action should be considered.

cluded specifically in other strategic planning techniques. This means that any differences in recommendations between the three classes could not be distinguished by these planning techniques. To show that this is a serious limitation, attention is turned to the recommendations derived from the three analyses.[56]

A number of recommendations that were made for improving the strategic posture of the benchmark case, analyzed in chapter 6, are not appropriate for the risk case shown in column 2 of table 7-2. Since this company mainly has difficulties with risk rather than with both risk and endurance, the recommendations tend to focus predominantly on risk-reducing items, although indirect benefits with respect to the other strategic elements will occur.

In particular, indirect benefits will accrue to strengthen even more the endurance of the company, as well as to improve the action range. Greater flexibility and a decrease in the requirements for precautionary liquidity should greet the shift of funds to SBUs with lower sales variability. A similar phenomenon can be expected if the operating leverage characteristics can be decreased. However, care must be taken that this action does not reduce the operating profit unduly. The proper shift of the geographic center of gravity to other areas and the project-oriented emphasis to the more profitable of the noncore activities will accelerate indirectly the improvement of all strategic elements, although the proposed actions are primarily directed at the improvement of the risk position.

It is significant that in this case, the company does not have to worry about slowing growth, shifting the allocation of funds to increase the velocity of the cash inflows, or changing the debt maturity structure. These changes would improve endurance and action range directly, but since there are no serious problems in these dimensions, focusing on the risk problem is called for instead. Deviating from the primary focus would be an inefficient use of resources and could lead to undesirable distortions in the opportunities sphere.

Thus rather significant differences in recommendations arise from the typological alterations in these two situations. These differences cannot, or not so effectively, be detected by most other planning techniques, so the conclusion must be that they tend to be of limited value regarding strategic completeness when used in the present context. This view is strengthened when recommendations for the endurance case in column 3 of table 7-2 are examined.

Column 3 of table 7-2 shows the striking parallelism between suggestions to improve action range and endurance. The action range in the endurance case is adequate—the firm under discussion commands sufficient long-run resources and capabilities to exploit opportunities selectively as they tend to arise. The problem is having the endurance to survive short-term shocks in order to enjoy the long run. More liquidity and higher cash inflow for the short term will strengthen both action range and endurance, so financial actions taken to improve endurance should have a direct, positive impact on action range, as far as the funding side of the latter is concerned, and vice versa.

It is also significant that for the endurance case, the exploitation of projects without outside partners is recommended. The benchmark case suggested either one or some selective joint ventures as an action that deserves priority consideration. The reasons are quite clear. Joint ventures can help to spread certain kinds of risk—mainly uncertainties inherent in individual SBUs or geographic areas. However, for broad, overall problems like endurance that encompass the whole firm—especially if the difficulties are as substantial as they are in the benchmark case—it is unrealistic to expect that joint venturing a small piece of the company can have much of a favorable impact.

It is also of importance in the endurance case to exercise more caution in exploiting growth opportunities. To maintain the initiative, the company under analysis must identify and concentrate resources in the most profitable areas. Failure to take these actions because of a preoccupation with the endurance problems can result in losing the initiative and increasing the risk to which the company is subjected.

The differences between the classifications in Resilience cases are brought about by the ability of PARE to discriminate between apparently only subtly different but in essence important characteristics. These distinctions become crucial when placed in the capital market context by a valuation framework and permit managers to shape their strategic responses to the environment. The three Resilience cases led to strongly divergent recommendations, but only because the analytical method employed had sufficient depth.[57] Simply defining the three cases broadly as risky cannot be guaranteed to yield situationally justified suggestions for action. For instance, selling off high-risk (but highly rewarding) projects when the difficulties are mainly with endurance might do more long-run harm than good.

Since the corporate portfolio techniques do not make appropriate distinctions in the Resilience perspective—indeed, most ignore this dimension—they cannot deal adequately with problems in PARE class III. These techniques do claim, however, to be able to give guidance predominantly from the perspective of Potential.

PROBLEMS FROM THE PERSPECTIVE OF POTENTIAL

PARE position II contains the three classes for Potential: mainly opportunities problems, mostly action range difficulties, and a combination of the two. Companies classified in one of these three categories exhibit a good Resilience position; hence strong typological differences would be expected between them and the benchmark case. Referring to table 7-3, the typification for the benchmark case is again shown in column 1, with all other columns keyed to it as in table

Table 7-3. Typifying Specifications for Firms with Potential and No Key Problems

		Typification Steps		*PARE IIIc: Problems with Risk and Endurance*
A.	1.	Market share	Core	Similar
			Noncore	Similar
		Market growth	Core	Similar
			Noncore	Rel. higher
	2.	Familiarity	Markets	Familiar
			Technology	Ongoing new
	3.	Knowledge and skill	Generalized	More than needed
			Specific marketing	Balanced
			Specific product qualities	Balanced
B.	4.	Cash-flow margin		Similar
	5.	Cash-flow balancing	Long-term cash release	Good
			Short-term cash release	Low
			Capacity for financing	Similar
C.	6.	Cash-flow growth	Core	Rel. higher
			Noncore	Similar
		Sales growth	Core	Rel. higher
			Noncore	Rel. higher
	7.	Concentration	Cash flow	Concentrated
			Sales	Concentrated
D.	8.	Economic circumstances	Main areas	Unfavorable
			Other areas	Good
	9.	Environmental change	Main area of core	None
			Main areas of noncore	Small favorable
	10.	Inflation impact on profitability	Inflation rate	Rel. higher
			Impact on cash flow	Greater on costs

PARE IIa: Problems Mainly with Opportunities	*PARE IIb: Problems Mainly with Action Range*	*PARE IIc: Problems with Opportunities and Action Range*	*PARE I: No Key Problems*
Rel. higher	–	Rel. higher	Rel. higher
–	Rel. lower	Rel. lower	–
Rel. lower	–	Rel. lower	Similar
Rel. lower	–	Similar	–
–	Ongoing new	Ongoing new	Ongoing new
–	Radically new	Radically new	–
Balanced	Balanced	Balanced	–
More than needed	Less than needed	Less than needed	–
More than needed	Less than needed	Less than needed	–
–	Rel. lower	Rel. lower	Rel. higher
Low	–	Low	Primary
Primary	High	Primary	Low requirements
–	Rel. lower	Rel. lower	Rel. higher
Rel. lower	Rel. lower	Rel. lower	–
–	–	Rel. lower	–
Similar	Similar	Similar	–
Similar	Similar	Similar	–
Dominant	Dominant	Dominant	Dominant
Dominant	Dominant	Dominant	Dominant
–	Good	–	Highly favorable
–	–	–	–
–	Small favorable	Large unfavorable	Large favorable
–	–	–	–
Similar	Similar	Similar	Similar
Similar	Similar	Similar	Greater on revenues

Table 7-3. continued

				PARE IIIc: Problems with Risk and Endurance
		Typification Steps		
E.	11.	Operating profitability		Similar
		Operating risk		Rel. higher
	12.	Bankruptcy chance	Fixed-charge coverage	Rel. lower
			Operating leverage	Similar
			Sales variability	Rel. higher
	13.	Insolvency chance	Debt maturity structure	More short term
			Liquidity	Rel. lower
			Cash-flow variability	Rel. higher
	14.	Weathering ability	Dividend coverage	Rel. lower
			Total leverage	Similar
			Sales variability	Rel. higher

Note: A dash signifies that the classification is the same as for the benchmark case.

7-1. The firm portrayed in column 4, with both opportunities and action range problems, is called the Potential case.

The only similarities between the benchmark case and the Potential case are with respect to the small, favorable, environmental change in the main geographic areas of the noncore SBUs and the economic circumstances in all areas (mostly unfavorable in the main geographic areas and mainly good in the other areas). The typification steps in the last two groups—D and E—plus concentration, having implications predominantly for the Resilience of the firm, are much more favorable for the Potential case than for the benchmark case. On the other hand, the first six typification steps, having primarily Potential ramifications, are uniformly weaker and less favorable for the Potential case than for the benchmark case. Thus, there are radical differences between the typification of the two departure situations.

Both the opportunities case (column 2 of table 7-3) and the action range case (column 3) have substantially better Resilience positions than the benchmark case has. On the Potential side, however, the signals are mixed. For the opportunities case, the important action range factors are satisfactory and usually

PARE IIa: Problems Mainly with Opportunities	*PARE IIb: Problems Mainly with Action Range*	*PARE IIc: Problems with Opportunities and Action Range*	*PARE I: No Key Problems*
Rel. lower	–	Rel. lower	Rel. higher
Rel. lower	Similar	Similar	–
Similar	Similar	Rel. higher	Rel. higher
–	–	Rel. lower	–
Similar	Similar	Similar	–
Similar	Similar	Similar	Similar
Similar	Similar	Similar	Rel. higher
Similar	Similar	Similar	Similar
Similar	Similar	Rel. higher	Rel. higher
–	–	Rel. lower	–
Similar	Similar	Similar	–

better than for the benchmark case. In terms of share-growth categories, the core and noncore SBUs fall mainly in the area of cash cows; they have relatively higher or similar market share and relatively lower market growth. The low long-term cash release and the excess specific marketing and product qualities knowledge and skill also indicate maturing opportunities.

It is likely that the standard share-growth analysis would also indicate in this case that the company has a problem with opportunities; there is a need to generate and promote new stars. However, the only reason that the share-growth approach came to the same conclusions as the PARE method is that the firm has relative strength in the other three strategic elements. Possible shortcomings of the share-growth procedure to identify adequately Potential problems can be shown in the action range.

The core activity in the action range case is clearly a cash cow, and the noncore activities are mainly question marks. The share-growth approach would recommend that the question marks be "quit or doubled", but it offers insufficient guidance on how to select from among the alternatives or about the ability of the firm to exploit any of the question marks with greater intensity and concentration than the others. PARE reveals that in this case there are significant difficulties with radically new technology and a lack of adequate marketing and product qualities knowledge and skill. Also the flexibility to act is restricted by a relatively lower cash-flow margin and the capacity for financing. Until these problems are confronted and relieved—and the usual share-growth analysis tends to ignore them—the company is not able to make sensible judgments about which question marks to "double".[58] It is possible—even likely—that the noncore activity with the most attractive long-term return prospects should not be "quit" or divested, but at the same time it cannot be "doubled" or intensified until the personnel problems are resolved. Primary attention to action range considerations will enable the company to achieve a stronger foundation for making important strategic decisions about which opportunities to exploit intensively.

The directional policy matrix approaches are capable, in principle, of dealing with these action range considerations in an appropriate way. Thus, they represent an improvement over the share-growth diagram. Similarly the Pethia and Saïas methodology[59] and that of Lorange[60] represent significant improvements—assuming that the firm does not also have underlying Resilience problems. If Resilience difficulties exist, all of these techniques offer—from the viewpoint of strategic completeness—inadequate guidance.

Table 7-4 shows that the recommendations for the three PARE II cases exhibit much less divergence than is shown for the Resilience cases. There are, however, some very important distinctions.[61] The Potential case concentrates on recommendations to focus more attention on the internal development (by such activities as research and development) or external acquisition of opportunities. The same type of concentration is suggested to acquire needed knowledge, skills, and technology, including the possibility of joint ventures and outright acquisition of other companies. Since the general economic circumstances in the main geographic areas are unfavorable and a large unfavorable change is expected further on, it is also advised that it is opportune to milk the core SBU even more by accelerating the cash inflow and minimizing the cash outflow for this activity as much as possible, thus shifting the allocation of funds away from such high-risk SBUs.

The opportunities case (column 5 of table 7-4) is analogous to the Potential case as far as recommendations to improve opportunities are concerned. However, since the noncore SBUs have mostly relatively lower market growth prospects, the possibilities for joint ventures to improve the opportunities outlook are worth investigating. The company has adequate competence, in fact a surplus of talent and financial resources, so the action-range-related recommendations are preventative. That is, the firm should exploit the core SBU more intensely and start a cost reduction program to prevent deterioration of the cash-flow margin. This step is necessary since sales are growing faster than cash flow.

An interesting observation is possible when the action range case is scrutinized. The close linkages between action range and endurance were shown when the endurance case was discussed, and the recommendations highlighted a direct relationship between improvements in the two strategic elements. Notice, however, that in column 6 of table 7-4, nothing is recommended to improve the action range that is of direct application to the endurance-action range link. The reason for this absence—notwithstanding their financial coherence—highlights an important distinction between the two strategic elements.[62]

In this action range case, the difficulties are caused not by problems with financial (cash) resources but by the lack of knowledge, skill, and technology. Endurance problems are primarily of a financial nature, so since the action range difficulties here are particularly nonfinancial, endurance-directed suggestions cannot attack the cause of the firm's problem. In this case, the improvement of the action range will have little if any benefit—even indirectly—for the endurance of the company.

Table 7-4 reveals the extent of differences between the three Resilience cases (columns 1-3) and the Potential cases (columns 4-6). Analytical techniques that do not make adequate distinctions between Potential and Resilience, or that ignore or treat superficially the Resilience side, cannot tailor the recommendations to meet the needs of the departure situation.[63] Thus, they can lead to unjustified generalizations. This danger is demonstrated vividly when the PARE I case (the last column of tables 7-3 and 7-4) is compared with the benchmark case.

The benchmark case was evaluated in chapter 6, and it was determined that the company has strong opportunities, action range, and thus Potential. The last column of table 7-3 makes clear that the PARE I case represents even stronger Potential than the benchmark case. However, the PARE I case also has good Resilience.

Typification of the departure situation in the two example cases reveals that there are strategically important differences between the two. Nevertheless, it would be rather difficult for current planning techniques to differentiate between the two because they play down Resilience, and the primary differences are in terms of Resilience issues.[64] It is inconceivable that the recommendations for the benchmark case should be applied to the PARE I case or, even more importantly, vice versa.

Looking to the recommendations for the PARE I case in the last column of table 7-4, only three actions are suggested. Obviously the company must be doing many things right to attain the superior strategic posture it enjoys. The three recommendations serve only to ensure that worrisome trends or inappro-

Table 7-4. Summary of Recommendations from Example Cases

Recommendations	*PARE IIIc: Endurance and Risk Problems*	*PARE IIIa: Mainly Risk Problems*
POTENTIAL		
A. OPPORTUNITIES-RELATED RECOMMENDATIONS		
1. Increase efforts to generate high-growth opportunities		
2. Acquisition or merger to increase the opportunities		
3. Joint venture to increase the opportunities		
4. Increase marketing efforts to open new markets	*	*
5. Shift allocation of funds to innovation projects		
6. Change the firm's center of gravity		
7. Change the intensity of the firm's efforts		
8. Concentrate resources in the most profita-able areas		
9. Exploit opportunities individually		
B. ACTION RANGE-RELATED RECOMMENDATIONS		
1. Shift action range strategy to increase short-term cash available	*	
2. Accelerate the cash inflow of the core SBU		
3. Accelerate the cash inflows of the noncore SBUs	*	
4. Shift funds to high short-term cash release SBUs		
5. Initiate a cost-reduction program	*	
6. Buy needed knowledge, skill, and technology		
7. Acquisition or merger to acquire needed knowledge, skill, and technology		
8. Joint venture to acquire needed knowledge, skill, and technology		
RESILIENCE		
C. RISK-ORIENTED RECOMMENDATIONS		
1. Abandon or sell high-risk projects	**	**

PARE IIIb: Mainly Endurance Problems	*PARE IIc: Opportunities and Action Range Problems*	*PARE IIa: Mainly Opportunities Problems*	*PARE IIb: Mainly Action Range Problems*	*PARE I: No Key Problem*
	**	**		
	*	*		
		*		
	**	**	*	
	**	**	*	
	*	**		
	*		*	
**				
*			*	**
*			*	
*	*	*	*	
*				
*				
*	**	*	*	*
	**		**	
	*		*	
	*			
		*		

Table 7-4. continued

Recommendations	*PARE IIIc: Endurance and Risk Problems*	*PARE IIIa: Mainly Risk Problems*
2. Joint venture high-risk projects to spread the risk	**	*
3. Exercise more caution in exploiting growth opportunities	*	*
4. Revise the operating leverage characteristics of the firm		*
5. Change the firm's center of gravity to reduce risk	*	*
6. Shift allocation of funds to lower-risk SBUs	**	**
7. Shift allocation of funds from higher-risk SBUs	**	**
8. Shift funds to SBUs with lower cash-flow variability	**	**
9. Shift funds to SBUs with lower sales variability	**	
D. ENDURANCE-ORIENTED RECOMMENDATIONS		
1. Increase the short-term flexibility of the endurance strategy	**	
2. Shift funds to high short-term cash release SBUs	*	
3. Institute a cost-reduction program	**	
4. Change the center of gravity for endurance	*	
5. Revise the debt maturity structure	**	
6. Revise the debt-equity mix		*
7. Exercise more caution in exploiting opportunities	**	
8. Slow the exploitation of growth until better harmonization with endurance is achieved	**	

*This suggestion is viable and deserves consideration.

**This recommendation is very important and/or urgent and this action should be considered.

PARE IIIb: Mainly Endurance Problems	*PARE IIc: Opportunities and Action Range Problems*	*PARE IIa: Mainly Opportunities Problems*	*PARE IIb: Mainly Action Range Problems*	*PARE I: No Key Problem*
**				
	*	*		
				*
**				
**				
**				
*				
**				
*				
*				
**				

Table 7-5. Geographically Oriented Recommendations

	PARE IIIc: Problems with Both Risk and Endurance	*PARE IIIa: Problems Mainly with Risk*
1. Change the firm's center of gravity to a different geographic distribution	**	**
2. Change the intensity of the firm's efforts geographically	**	**
3. Shift the allocation of funds to the main geographic area of the core SBU		
4. Shift the allocation of funds to the main geographic areas of the noncore SBUs		
5. Shift the allocation of funds to the other geographic areas of the core SBU	**	**
6. Shift the allocation of funds to the other geographic areas of the noncore SBUs	*	*
7. Remove funds from the main geographic area of the core SBU	**	**
8. Remove funds from the main geographic areas of the noncore SBUs	*	*
9. Remove funds from the other geographic areas of the core SBU		
10. Remove funds from the other geographic areas of the noncore SBUs		

*This suggestion is viable and deserves consideration.

**This recommendation is very important and/or urgent and this action should be considered.

priate actions do not weaken the position in the long run. First, the company is in such a favorable state that exploiting opportunities individually is called for. Why dilute the profitability of ventures by taking on partners? The firm under study is also in good risk position and can afford to take—if need be—somewhat more risk to gain good returns. For the benchmark case, on the other hand, joint ventures of high-risk projects to spread the unfavorable consequences of the uncertainty involved are strongly recommended.

The other two suggestions in the PARE I case reflect the fact that, in common with the benchmark case, there is relatively higher sales variability and the sales growth rate is higher than the cash-flow growth rate. Thus initiating a pro-

PARE IIIb: Problems Mainly with Endurance	*PARE IIc: Problems with Opportunities and Action Range*	*PARE IIa: Problems Mainly with Opportunities*	*PARE IIb: Problems Mainly with Action Range*	*PARE I: No Key Problems*
*	**	**		
*	**	*		
*				
*				
	**			
	*	*		
	*	**		*
*		*		
*				

gram to reduce costs (and thus improve the cash flow over time) and a shift of funds to SBUs with lower sales variability to reduce risk is probably appropriate for both items.

Clearly, however, the recommendations for the PARE I case will not help the company in the benchmark case. In fact if a preoccupation with individual action is pursued, the risk dimension of the benchmark case could deteriorate further. Thus inadequate typological structure from both the Potential and the Resilience perspectives can lead to unjustified generalizations and recommendations for action that can do more harm than good.

The weak signals about possible future problems identified in the PARE I case are also significant. It is reasonable to suppose that the direction given by these weak signals would be more difficult to acquire in a timely manner with the current planning techniques. It is also less likely with these techniques that appropriate actions could be forthcoming to counter the trends implied by their existence before the trends are more manifest.[65] This advantage of the preplanning method presented here is important considering the trend to an increasing complexity and changeability in the business environment.

GEOGRAPHIC IMPLICATIONS

To demonstrate another strength of the PARE-based typification methodology over other planning techniques, recommendations can be provided from the geographic field of view. In table 7-5, applicable suggestions from all example cases have been extracted and arrayed from the geographic perspective. These could be further subdivided by opportunities, action range, risk, and endurance, but for the illustrative purpose at hand, it was not considered to be necessary. Notice also in this table that there are no geographically oriented recommendations for the PARE IIb case. Reference to the departure situation in table 7-3 for this example case will reveal why this is logical and correct.

The ability to give specific geographic recommendations is particularly important in today's changing world in which many firms operate in more than a single area. Most of the other planning techniques either pay inadequate attention to the geographic aspect or treat it outside of the main planning technique.[66] Integration of this dimension in the main analysis can yield richer and strategically more meaningful recommendations for appropriate actions. This is particularly true when the PARE and BIM approaches are used jointly on the basis of the typological approach.[67] In this case, there is a tendency for more relevant, timely, and situationally balanced recommendations, with less cause for doubt about their strategic appropriateness, than is true with the less comprehensive planning techniques.

If, as a result of the PARE-based analysis, other more problem-specific features require an additional investigation, it is also possible to conduct this inquiry in a well-grounded way. This ability to increase the depth of analysis on a specific problem, while remaining within the confines of the same analytical framework, is of great importance in promoting consistency. Such a problem-oriented follow-up approach to specific geographic topics is presented in the next chapter.

8 FOLLOW-UP SITUATIONAL TYPIFICATION

The overall typification method should not be too elaborate in order to prevent unnecessary complexity. A careful selection of fourteen steps has been made to characterize the most important dimensions of a company's departure situation. This implies that the introductory typification, though rather comprehensive, is sometimes still too general to give recommendations for all relevant dimensions, considering the various problems that a firm could encounter. Especially for determining detailed actions for strategic improvement and the associated implementation issues in case of a particular problem, a follow-up is needed. This follow-up cannot be given here in an encyclopedic way since each peculiar problem requires additional information and has to be considered on its own merits. Therefore the discussion is confined to an extended treatment of a distinctive problem—internationalization—to illustrate how such issues can be approached effectively. The typification process is demonstrated with the help of two example cases, both dealing with companies considering further international expansion but for different reasons.

INTERNATIONALIZATION TO REDUCE RISK

The first example is a firm that is situated in PARE position IIIa; it has weak Resilience because of mainly risk problems. The overall typification of the

Geographic Breakdown of the Firm's Activities							
A	B	C	D	E	F	G	H
40	20	10	8	8	5	5	4

Figure 8-1. Distribution of Total Net Cash Flow over Geographic Areas (in percent)

company's departure situation has revealed that there are no substantial problems with respect to opportunities, action range, and endurance but that the risk level is unacceptably high. For illustration purposes, it is supposed that this example is the risk case presented and elucidated in tables 7-1 and 7-2. From this initial analysis, preliminary recommendations could be extracted, but further typification steps are required to ascertain and specify the right actions, including implementation suggestions, to improve the unfavorable posture. Thus the root causes of the firm's risk problem have to be examined first.

Further characterization factors beyond the ones already used in the preparatory typification must be considered. An indication of the nature of such additional factors can usually be found by careful reflection on the results of the overall typification and the introductory suggestions extracted from it. In the case under review, there is direct evidence that the risk problem is geographically oriented. Since attention was drawn to shifting the emphasis to other areas as preliminary advice for possible improvement, it is useful to investigate further whether this geographic shift should be recommended.

In the overall typification, some geographically oriented steps have already been incorporated to characterize broadly the firm's current SBUs: economic circumstances, environmental change, and inflation impact on profitability. In addition, further typification in the geographic perspective is required.

The first question to be answered in such a follow-up is how the firm's current SBUs are spread over the discernible geographic areas. As a measure for each SBU, sales, cash flow, or even the total sum of capital invested can be used to determine the spread. Throughout the book, cash flow has been regarded as the most salient factor to consider so it will be used for this purpose. The SBUs of the company in the risk case are assumed to operate in eight different geographic areas (A-H) and the total net cash flow is distributed among them as shown in figure 8-1.

The next question to be answered is what other characteristics of the geographic areas covered by the firm's current SBUs are most relevant. A selection of other important geographic attributes leads to the following supplementary list:

Investment climate refers to management's evaluation of the attitude toward business in the geographic area under consideration (for more specifics, see glossary item 30).

Geographic risk deals with management's perception of the geographically oriented risk (political, economic, and sociological, for example) as far as it affects the net cash flow of the projects executed in the area under analysis (glossary item 50).

Cash-flow transferability refers to the extent to which host governments place restrictions on the movement of generated profits to other units of the firm outside the host country (glossary item 8).

Geographic cash-flow variability is the perceived extent to which the net cash flow from the projects within the geographic area under study tends to fluctuate as approached by the coefficient of variation of the cash flow calculated over the most recent five-year period (glossary item 58).

Geographic cash-flow growth rate indicates the annual compound rate of increase in net cash flow available to the firm from the geographic area under review (glossary item 22).

Geographic market growth rate refers to the annual compound rate of growth in total demand for the products or services provided by the firm's activities within the area under study (glossary item 24).

Accessibility for cash-flow anticipation deals with the extent to which management has confidence in its ability to forecast accurately the expected future cash flow anticipated to come from the SBUs in the geographic area under analysis (glossary item 2).

Some of the factors mentioned are partly overlapping; however, it is very difficult to compose a set of mutually exclusive variables without the danger of neglecting some important aspects. Management can rate each of these factors on a five-point scale for all eight geographic areas pertinent to the current SBUs. For example, environmental change may be evaluated according to the following classification categories: radically favorable, ongoing favorable, no appreciable impact, ongoing unfavorable, and radically unfavorable.

As a reference point, the country is chosen, from all countries in which the company or its reference firm are active, that has an average or median value with respect to the attribute under consideration. The reference country may sometimes be different for various attributes, depending upon the specific nature of the factor under discussion.

To each classification category pertinent to the aspect under review, a value on a Likert-type continuum between 1 and 5 is assigned; 1 corresponds to the most favorable rank, in terms of impact on cash flow, and 5 is the most unfavorable. If management assesses the characteristic of a country under study as identical to the corresponding attribute of the relevant reference country, a score of 3 is assigned to that characteristic. In this way, one can compute a weighted average score for the firm as a whole for each factor by multiplying the cash-flow percentages from figure 8-1 with the scores associated with the appropriate rank. This is demonstrated for geographic risk in table 8-1.

For the example case, the company's average score on geographic risk as a whole is rather high—3.8—compared to the median score of 3.0. However, such numerical values are meant only as rough indications for comparative purposes, so too much significance should not be attached to their apparent exactness. Computing the scores for the firm as a whole in tables such as table 8-1 has the advantage of giving visible insight into how these scores are derived; the calculation procedure itself often contains important information. Furthermore, such tables permit a comprehensive approach in case the characteristic differs between areas with respect to the discernible activities exploited therein. In this manner, the firm's average scores can be determined for all attributes that are considered to be important for further typification of the follow-up analysis. For the company in the example case, the values presented in table 8-2 were computed for the previously mentioned characterization factors.

This way of characterizing the firm's attributes by means of numerical scores has the advantage of giving further insight into the current situation and its

Table 8-1. Comparative Scores: Risk Perception of the Geographic Areas

Geographic Riskiness Rank	*Cash Flow Percentages per Country*[a] *A*	*B*	*C*	*D*	*E*	*F*	*G*	*H*	*Weighted Score*
Very low 1			10						10 × 1 = 10
Low 2							5		5 × 2 = 10
Medium 3				8					8 × 3 = 24
High 4	40					5		4	49 × 4 = 196
Very high 5		20			8				28 × 5 = 140
Total									380
Average score									3.8

[a]Currently covered countries.

strengths and weaknesses, keeping in mind that 3.0 is the median value. It has been assumed that a high score for each attribute corresponds to an unfavorable impact on net cash flow. Thus table 8-2 shows that the company is apparently concentrated in geographic areas in which the economic circumstances are worse than average, in which the investment climate is not very good, and for which the risk characteristics are rather unfavorable. Also, the perceived change in the business environment is expected to be less favorable than average. The positive factors, such as cash-flow transferability and cash-flow growth rate, do not outweigh the negative ones. Four factors are considered to be similar to their respective counterparts in the reference country.

This follow-up analysis confirms the preliminary finding that was derived from the introductory identification.[68] The firm should certainly shift the emphasis to one or more of the other geographic areas, provided that such a change in the international center of gravity is strategically adapted to the specific situation under review. Considering the firm's strategic posture, this spread of interests should be risk reducing, provided that the corresponding returns are sufficiently rewarding. This consideration has important implications with respect to both the activity chosen for expansion abroad and the countries in which such internationalization should be effected. On the one hand, the company in these circumstances has to refrain from radically new activities, since the lack of experience would be too great a risk. Therefore, it is recommended that the expansion abroad be in terms of an extension of the core business or an activity closely related to it. On the other hand, to effect further internationalization, countries should be chosen that have favorable characteristics regarding their ability to improve the unhealthy risk position.

Additional information about the required qualities of countries to be selected

Table 8-2. Characterization Scores for the Risk Case

Characterization Factor	*Score*
Economic circumstances	3.8
Environmental change	3.1
Inflation impact	3.0
Investment climate	3.2
Geographic risk	3.8
Cash-flow transferability	2.8
Geographic cash-flow variability	3.0
Geographic cash-flow growth rate	2.5
Geographic market growth rate	3.0
Accessibility for cash-flow anticipation geographically	3.0

will be supplied in the follow-up typification described below. In this respect, one should take care that the intended international expansion for purposes of risk reduction will not have a damaging impact on the firm's favorable departure position according to the other three strategic elements.

In preparing for the selection of countries, one should gather information about salient characteristics of the areas that are viable candidates. This process preceding the location decision is called *geographic specification.* For this specification, all geographic attributes that were dealt with in the follow-up typification have to be considered in analyzing the pros and cons of the candidate countries. Additionally, however, this group of factors should be supplemented by characteristics that reflect the impact of the intended internationalization on the strategic elements of opportunities, action range, and endurance.

The overall typification revealed that there are no problems with these other strategic elements, but it is necessary to protect that favorable position so that the risk problem will not be replaced by another one—for instance, an action range problem. In this context, management must choose a key attribute for each of these strategic elements that is useful as a relevant signal for preventing unfavorable developments. It is assumed that in the example firm, the following key factors have been identified as being particularly useful for this safeguarding function:

1. A geographically oriented version of the operating profitability/operating risk feature for monitoring the opportunities dimension (glossary items 42 and 52, respectively).

2. Capital requirements for the geographic area under review for scanning action range as well as endurance problems resulting from the scarcity of capital.

Therefore an adequate set of factors for the process of geographic specification is the following:

1. Economic circumstances.
2. Environmental change.
3. Inflation impact.
4. Investment climate.
5. Geographic risk.
6. Cash-flow transferability.
7. Geographic cash-flow variability.
8. Geographic cash-flow growth rate.
9. Geographic market growth rate.
10. Accessibility of cash-flow anticipation geographically.

11. Operating profitability/operating risk geographically.
12. Capital requirements.

Returning to the company in the example case, the follow-up typification clearly demonstrated that further expansion abroad is appropriate for mitigating the firm's risk problem. It is assumed that the strategic position under study cannot be improved substantially by timely retrenchment of the most vulnerable activities in above-average risk countries because of social, economic, and political factors. It is also presumed that the firm has already chosen an appropriate activity for international expansion and it now faces the problem of where to construct the new facility.

For illustrative purposes, the problem is confined to a situation in which there are three countries remaining after preselection on obvious characteristics. At first sight, there do not seem to be enough differences in attractiveness to make a clear-cut decision among the three. Thus, a geographic specification is needed, adapted to the problem situation under consideration, to make the choice. For the three remaining countries, the information contained in table 8-3 is available.

Aided by the geographic specification, the structured evaluation of the "where" decision is made significantly easier.[69] The prevailing criterion is the reduction of the firm's total risk by additional internationalization, so country Z is the least suitable of the three. In evaluating the pros and cons of the other two countries, the firm's scores in the follow-up typification should be kept in mind. The economic circumstances in the present geographic areas covered by the firm are rather unfavorable, so country X, which may improve the company's score on this important characteristic, is a prime candidate.

Having considered the direct impact of additional foreign opreations on the risk position of the firm—the strategic element that is primarily applicable—attention should also be paid to the indirect impacts of international expansion on the other strategic elements. In this respect, country Y, with a better operating profitability than country X, is slightly superior, but both countries are suitable from the point of view of the impact on opportunities, action range, and endurance. Since country X has the superior risk position, the slight return sacrifice is considered to be acceptable.

The supplemental typification justifies the choice of country X on both a relevant and on a comprehensive basis. This discriminating power is one of the achievements of the methodology presented in this book. Therefore, since in the example case it is clear that choosing country X for internationalization will improve the risk position and will not harm the other strategic elements, it is recommended that the firm extend the core business (or an activity closely related to it) into country X.

As a contrast to this risk issue, a case will be examined of a company that

Table 8-3. Geographic Specification for the Remaining Three Alternative Countries

Specification Factors	*X*	*Y*	*Z*
Economic circumstances	Good	Medium	Good
Environmental change	No appreciable	Ongoing favorable	Ongoing favorable
Inflation impact	Low favorable	No appreciable	No appreciable
Investment climate	Similarly attractive	Similarly attractive	Highly attractive
Geographic risk	Low	Low	High
Cash-flow transferability	No problems	Relatively lower	No problems
Geographic cash-flow variability	Average	Average	More than average
Geographic cash-flow growth rate	Moderate	Good	Good
Geographic market growth rate	Moderate	Good	Good
Accessibility for cash-flow anticipation geographically	Average	Good	Average
Operating profitability/operating risk geographically	Moderate/low	Good/moderate	Good/high
Capital requirements	Medium	Medium	High

must cope with an opportunities problem. As in the first example, a follow-up typification is required. In the second case, the indications for actions to improve the unfavorable posture are more ambiguous after the initial overall typification than they were in the first example. Thus the follow-up typification will require more analytical depth.

INTERNATIONALIZATION TO IMPROVE OPPORTUNITIES

The second example case is a company in PARE posture IIa. Thus it has a good position with regard to action range, risk, and endurance, but it has problems with opportunities. If the present strategy is continued, there will be insufficient opportunities in which this company can invest profitably in the near future. To find the root cause of this problem and to develop the appropriate strategy to get out of this unfavorable strategic posture, a follow-up typification is needed. It begins with a close examination of the information supplied by the general typification, supplemented by a number of additional steps that can throw more light on the problem situation under consideration. As in the first example case, some indications can be found with the help of the overall typification about the direction in which these incremental steps should proceed.

In this case, there are two different indications that require attention as a consequence of the introductory typification presented in chapter 7. First, it seems that the core activity is in the declining phase of the product life cycle and that insufficient focus has been given to the development of new products that can replace it. Second, there is an indication that inadequate thought has been devoted to finding new investment opportunities in current activities in other geographic areas with high market growth possibilities. Therefore, the follow-up typification in this second case will be much more extensive than in the previous one, which had only direct evidence for just one direction of strategic improvement.

Beyond the geographic aspects mentioned earlier, a number of product attributes should be included:

Operating leverage by projects measures the impact of a change in sales on earnings before interest and tax for the project under study (glossary item 32).

Product price indicates the relative categorization of the selling price of the relevant product(s) or service(s) under review into market segments labeled as "high priced", "low priced", and so forth (glossary item 38).

Product quality refers to the assessment by management of the relative categorization of the quality of the relevant product(s) or services(s) into market segments referred to as "high quality", "low quality", and so forth (glossary item 39).

Operating profitability/operating risk (by project) deals with a relative consideration of the operating profitability index and the operating risk of the project(s) under study (glossary items 41 and 51, respectively).

Technology implications relates, for the activities under review, comparative indications regarding technology sophistication and technology change indication to relative impressions of technology familiarity. Technology sophistication refers to the relative distance from the state of the art of applicable technology development in conjunction with the degree of complexity in utilizing the technology (glossary item 55). Technology change indication deals with the likelihood of changes in technology (glossary item 53). Technology familiarity means the extent to which management has confidence in its experience and ability to utilize the firm's expertise with respect to the technology required to be competitive in the market of the project(s) under study (glossary item 44).

Business cost stance of projects refers to the combination of the inflation sensitivity of business costs of activities (glossary item 28) and the joint impact of economies of scale and learning curve economies for the project(s) under consideration (glossary items 15 and 14, respectively).

Revenue posture by project(s) relates the revenue stance of the project(s) to the impact of inflation on the net revenue of the activities in the geographic area(s) under analysis. This stance indicates the relative position of the firm's project(s) under study in comparison with the relevant competitor concerning the ability to utilize marketing and technology skill, learning curve economies, economies of scale, and any other factor to enhance the net revenue in question (glossary item 48). The inflation impact on net revenue is determined by management reflection on the differential effect of inflation on project revenues (glossary item 29) and on business cost (glossary item 28).

Management has to evaluate all projects exploited by the company with respect to these product characteristics. Thus in this case, the applicable follow-up typification is much more comprehensive since it is based on a broader collection of both product-oriented and geographic attributes.[70] It will be assumed here that, after careful analysis of actual aspects, management of the example firm concludes that the opportunities problem is not primarily due to the composition of the firm's product range.

Reflection on the geographic side of the follow-up typification, however, leads to strong indications that the current regions do not contain sufficient opportunities that can be exploited profitably in the near term. The consensus in the firm under study is that there is little use or no time to develop new products for the present markets. Therefore, as in the first example case, a shift of emphasis to other geographic areas is indicated—but from a divergent perspective.

In this case, the underlying motive for internationalization—the development of new markets to relieve the opportunities problem—has specific consequences for establishing the criterion for judging the intended improvement and its implementation.[71] With respect to the activity to be chosen for going international, choice of the core activity or a related one is not so critical since the risk position of the example company is rather strong, considering its PARE posture. However, since insufficient attention appears to have been given in the past to research and development for product innovation, it is assumed that for the intended international spread, an activity is chosen that is a modified version of the firm's core SBU.

Having some strategic latitude regarding risk characteristics with respect to the country to be chosen, the main purpose is to find an area with good opportunities prospects. More indications in the geographic context can be extracted from the applicable follow-up typification. A supplementary consideration is the impact of the international expansion under study on the corporate position according to the other three strategic elements: action range, risk, and endurance. The departure situation reveals a favorable picture in these respects, and the implementation of international spread for better opportunities should be compatible with safeguarding this beneficial stance.

With these considerations in mind, an evaluation of the attributes of the candidate countries can be started. For illustration purposes, it is again assumed that with respect to the internationalization under review, the three countries X, Y, and Z specified in table 8-3 remain after preselection on obvious characteristics. Careful analysis of the geographic specification for these three countries indicates that country X is least suitable for the prime purpose of improving the opportunities position. The expected market, cash flow, and profitability prospects are only moderate. This is sufficient reason to drop country X as a candidate.

The choice between countries Y and Z is very close. An investment in country Z is riskier than in country Y, but since the risk position of the company is rather strong, this is not a dominant factor. Also the differences with respect to the investment climate and the capital requirements need not be decisive because the somewhat more attractive investment climate does not necessarily lead to a higher profit expectation, and the firm's action range is sufficiently strong to cope with eventual problems in this respect. It seems that the deciding factor in this situation will be a superficially unimportant difference between Y and Z: the cash-flow transferability of generated profits.

To clarify this point, reference is made to the overall typification of the opportunities case at hand presented in tables 7-3 and 7-4. The analysis of this departure situation showed that the adequate endurance position of the example firm at present is at least partially due to the absence of high growth opportunities. A warning is indicated from this that an increased emphasis on generating and exploiting opportunities might precipitate a deterioration of the endurance. Therefore, the transferability of cash flow from new investment areas should be good to mitigate the development of future endurance problems.

This indication makes the choice of country Y, from which cash flow can only be transferred to other countries with difficulty, less suitable. Since very strict legal regulations regarding the ownership aspects of companies are often intertwined with transferability problems—especially in developing countries—this consideration becomes even more important. In country Z there are probably no restrictions of this nature; perhaps this is one of the reasons that the investment climate is more attractive than in the other two countries. Further, in country Z, the firm will encounter no problems regarding cash-flow transferability. The conclusion is that country Z is most suitable for international expansion.

Thus, when comparing the two example cases for a similar implementation problem, quite divergent countries emerge as the prime candidate. These two illustrations demonstrate that even in very singular problem situations, the method presented in this book has discriminating power.

9 PROSPECTIVE TRACKING OF THE PROJECT SET

Strategic analysis requires the focusing of attention on the expected future path of evolution of a company. This means that the dynamics of the environment and the firm's reaction to change must be considered explicitly if strategically valid suggestions are to emerge from the analysis. This philosophy has permeated the development of the PARE-based methodology described thus far, and at various points, explicit attention has been paid to it. However, to draw together the various strategic aspects into a dynamic synthesis, a prospective approach to identification of the direction in which the firm's project set is moving must be described.

Prospective tracking is the name given to this dynamics investigation method. When conducted in the framework of a strategic gap analysis, this approach can be used to project the ramifications of the PARE-based and BIM-checked indications. These projections can be used to reflect on whether the desired consequences are capable of being realized with the suggested actions. In this way help can be offered for discovering recommendations that are consistent with the needs of the current situation of the firm, are strategically balanced, and promote dynamically the desired outcome for the future. Thus, prospective tracking is an aid for following the historical and current trends in the company's operations and anticipating their development into at least the near term. Considering the inherent complexity and changeability in the corporate environment, this monitoring must be done frequently.

THE BASICS OF TRACKING

Tracking is defined as following the visible path left by the characteristic being monitored as it moves through time and space. In its simplest form, tracking implies the calculation of a value for the characteristic at various points in time and plotting the trend so obtained. If this type of tracking is conducted in a timely manner, it is possible to spot trends at an early stage either by visual inspection or by employing some quantitative device, such as time-series regression.

This type of tracking is widely advocated in conventional texts on financial analysis. However, for project set management, it is not wholly satisfactory. The past is irrelevant except as it gives insight to applicable cause-effect linkages. Thus, prospective tracking in at least the short term is required to provide management with the type of information they need to manage the project set.

Prospective tracking refers to projecting the characteristic under review into the future and following the trace thought to be the most likely, given the departure situation, the actions (or inactions) to be taken, and the probable environmental reaction. This does not imply a simple extrapolation of the past since it is based on the interpretation of implications of the current position of the feature under study and its expected future movement, mainly in terms of direction and possibly even the rough magnitude and rate of change.

Prospective tracking is employed to depict a firm's project set as it moves over time in order to identify its probable development in important perspectives. This permits early determination of trends and allows proper adaptive control adjustments to be made to ensure, as far as possible, that the strategic posture of the company continues to move in the intended direction in terms of the PARE space.

Selection of Reference Items

Tracking implies that it is possible to define the characteristic under study appropriately considering its purpose. The characteristic must also be stable over time and space with respect to the definition to permit valid intertemporal comparisons. Similarly it must be possible to determine by a consistent process a score for this characteristic, preferably a cardinal representation, which can be followed over time and the trend derived therefrom. A characteristic that meets these requirements is suitable for use in a so-called tracking level.

A tracking level is defined to be proportion calculated for a strategically important attribute and applicable to the whole of the company's project set, that, when monitored over a period of time, can reveal information about the degree of success that management has enjoyed in attaining or maintaining an advantageous position. In this respect, tracking levels are particularly worthwhile when used or evaluated in the PARE perspective. Therefore, they must either be anchored to a fixed reference point or associated with a well-defined classification scheme for reasons similar to those for the previously discussed typification steps. Four external reference items are proposed to be employed for defining various tracking levels.

1. The *reference firm* is the firm, preferably of similar size and product mix and operating in the same industry(ies) or in a related activity field, that is chosen by management as its corporate benchmark. Simultaneously this reference item must be classified as sound by the financial world in terms of the characteristics required to survive effectively in the actual environment. The use of the reference firm as a benchmark is most appropriate when it is desired to specify a tracking level representing the company under discussion.

2. When, instead of on the corporation as a whole, the analysis is focused upon an SBU—a distinctive product line and its related markets—the adequate reference point is the *relevant competitor.* This competitor is the firm that management considers to be the prime competitor in the product-market field under study. Sometimes it may be the reference firm, but quite often it will be another company engaged as the dominant competitor in the activity under analysis.

3. The relevant *industrial sector* is used as the reference point when the tracking level is more appropriately keyed to either one or more industries in aggregate terms rather than to any particular company. Also, it is appropriate when the tracking level refers to a single aggregate industry out of all industries in which either the company or its reference firm is active.

4. Some tracking levels are more of a macroeconomic nature and thus cannot appropriately be benchmarked to another firm or even to an industrial sector. In this case, it is necessary to establish a *reference country.* This is the country having the most typical or normal value of the parameter under analysis from the set of all countries in which the company under review or its reference firm is active.

It is not realistic to assume that management is always able to ascertain in a reliable way the appropriate external reference item. Since benchmarks are still required, as an auxiliary approach they will then have to be based predominantly on the firm's internal information on the applicable category of activities that is available to management. Such classes refer to either one or more SBU(s), associated with either all, some, or one of its (their) geographic areas(s). These reference points are mainly determined by choosing the median of the distribution of the factor under discussion considering the category in question of the current projects of the company or of its reference firm. By also giving attention to the equivalent category of the reference firm, a strategically warranted orientation will be promoted grosso modo.

For some tracking levels, mainly internal reference points may be more appropriate than external references, but for others, the use of internal benchmarks represents a pragmatically necessary compromise considering the reliably available information. In this respect, a rough but consistent internal approach, externally relativized if at all possible, is better than nothing. The impact of such a compromise is lessened by the fact that the direction representing an improvement in the level under study and its significance can be ascertained independently of the specification of the reference point. Thus, as long as there is consistency in the choice of preferably guided internal reference items, the important objective of monitoring strategic improvement or deterioration in the management of the company's project set can reasonably be effected.

For a few tracking levels, the choice of a reference item would be so arbitrary as to render comparisons on this basis almost meaningless. Under these circumstances, a well-defined classification scheme is preferred to categorize a level adequately.

Specifying Scores for Tracking Levels

When selecting appropriate tracking levels, some strategically important characteristics are easier to specify and use than others. Some levels, such as the debt ratio or earnings per share, are simply calculated from generally available quantitative data. Other important tracking levels do not enjoy the same information availability, particularly when they represent qualitative factors that are difficult to estimate and to transform into meaningful comparisons. Nevertheless, such characteristics are often strategically very important so that a concentration of attention only upon easier-to-grasp data would be dangerous. The crux of the problem with qualitative or nearly intangible data is that they are very difficult to quantify meaningfully, and, without quantification, it is not feasible to include them in a structured manner in formal models of choice. It is possible, and in many instances even common, for managers to assign ordinal rankings to two or more data samples pertinent to some difficult-to-quantify characteristic. The exploitation of this property is the key to the inclusion in a meaningful way of much hard-to-grasp but crucial information for strategic preplanning.

The CONIC method (Cardinal Ordering of Near-Intangible Characteristics) provides the procedure for strategically converting qualitative data regarding individual activities into quantitative representations of significance for a firm's project set as a whole.[72] Supposing a reasonable reference item, a symmetric Likert-type classification scale and the ability of the manager to place reliably the firm's SBUs on the pertinent continuum according to an important characteristic of a qualitative nature, CONIC can be applied. Assume, for example, that the assessment scale relative to a suitable reference point consists of the comparative categories relatively higher, similar, and relatively lower. The ranking indication for the characteristic in question is then assessed separately for each current activity and investment proposal of the firm under analysis. Depending on the problem concerned, the initial ranking for each project can then be assigned some appropriate weight—for instance, for a resource allocation problem, the proper weights are mostly the capital expenditure required for the activity under review. Thereafter, sums of these individual project weights are taken for all activities falling within each of the three comparative categories. Dividing these sums per category by the total sum of all weights converts each of the three categorization sums into a weighted percentage of the firm's activities having that classification in question. These percentages are particularly meaningful for structuring the tracking and steering process.

The CONIC method can be applied equally well to inherently tangible and directly quantifiable information. By doing this, all types of information can be reduced to a common basis, thus stimulating more significant comparisons and better strategic preplanning.

Using Tracking Levels to Gain Insight

There are three ways that tracking levels can be used to gain insight into the strategic perspective of a company under study. Standing alone, a tracking level can yield important information about some aspect of corporate performance that is significant of and by itself. As an example, cash-flow transferability of generated profits was used as part of the follow-up typification in chapter 8 (glossary item 8). Using the CONIC method, this characterization factor can be converted into an important tracking level using the following classification categories: unrestricted, relatively higher, relatively lower, and zero transferability. As an aid in managing the project set, steering ratios can be formed and prospectively tracked to gauge the direction in which the firm is heading with respect to this factor. For instance, among others the following four steering ratios can be useful:

$$1.\ \text{Unrestricted transferability of generated profits} = \frac{\Sigma\ (\text{cash flow from the firm's SBUs within geographic areas with unrestricted transferability of generated profits})}{\Sigma\ (\text{cash flow from all current SBUs})}.$$

$$2.\ \text{Higher than average transferability of generated profits} = \frac{\Sigma\ (\text{cash flow from the firm's SBUs within geographic areas with either unrestricted or relatively higher transferability of generated profits})}{\Sigma\ (\text{cash flow from all current SBUs})}.$$

$$3.\ \text{Lower than average transferability of generated profits} = \frac{\Sigma\ (\text{cash flow from the firm's SBUs within geographic areas with either relatively lower or zero transferability of generated profits})}{\Sigma\ (\text{cash flow from all current SBUs})}.$$

$$4.\ \text{Zero transferability of generated profits} = \frac{\Sigma\ (\text{cash flow from the firm's SBUs within geographic areas with zero transferability of generated profits})}{\Sigma\ (\text{cash flow from all current SBUs})}.$$

If this factor is considered as one of the more important influences on geographic risk, the higher the first two steering ratios (and the lower the last two), the lower tends to be the risk. Thus, in this dimension, tracking the value of the steering ratios over time and at least into the near future will reveal the prospective development of this influence on the type of risk under study for the company as a whole. If developments are unsatisfactory, steps can be taken to adjust accordingly.

For many of the tracking levels, absolute measures can be calculated that have meaning in addition to and apart from the relative measure. When appropriate, these absolute measures will augment the relative levels so as to utilize fully all available and applicable information.

It may also be possible to increase the depth of the strategic picture by realizing that several individual levels may offer a different perspective of the same general concept. These related tracking levels can be grouped together to form a family of tracking levels. In this way, a multidimensional representation of the underlying concept emerges that yields a greater depth of meaning in a way analogous to that of a holograph giving greater visual depth. An example of such a family would be the tracking levels corresponding to the geographically oriented factors presented in table 8-3. Prospectively tracked, this family can shed light on the geographic characteristics as they unfold over time.

Another class of tracking levels is formed by combining individual tracking levels into *combilevels* (combinations of individual tracking levels), which can facilitate an increase of insight into the strategic situation by the juxtaposition of several worthwhile concepts into a single summary indicator. Combilevels are designed to create a synergistic effect whereby the insight available to the manager is increased over that available from the individual levels considered separately.

Since combilevels are particularly important for project set tracking, three representative examples are discussed. The first is the technology implications survey. For the SBUs under study, it relates the technology sophistication (glossary item 55) and technology change indication (item 53) to technology familiarity (item 54). Once the individual levels have been estimated for each SBU, the appropriate cell of table 9-1 can be determined. After all SBUs have been so classified, the initial entries in each cell represent the sum of the capital requirements (the weights) for SBUs falling within that cell. Since these data are then divided by the total capital requirements of all SBUs, the resulting entry in each cell is the percentage of total current SBUs for that cell.

Using the estimates according to table 9-1, data aggregated from the following groups of numbered cells can be particularly important as steering ratios for managing the project set:

Radically new features for the firm = 1 + 2 + 3 + 4 + 5 + 6 + 7 + 8 + 9.

Ongoing new features = 10 + 11 + 12 + 13 + 14 + 15 + 16 + 17 + 18.

New features with high change technology = 1 + 10 + 4 + 13.

Nonroutine and high-change technology = 1 + 10 + 19 + 4 + 13 + 22.

Familiar projects with stable technology = 21 + 24 + 27.

Since each cell represents the percentage of the total project set falling within that cell, these steering ratios are also the percentage of the current projects having the summary characteristic under review. Tracking these five—or any other combination—sets of values from a prospective point of view can identify trends as to the technology complexion of the firm, at least in the near future.[73] This is especially important for companies in so-called high-technology fields to en-

Table 9-1. Projects' Technological Implications Indication

Corporate Technology Familiarity Regarding Projects	*Advanced Technology Sophistication*			*Ongoing Nonroutine Technology Sophistication*			*Routine Technology Sophistication*		
	Technological Change			*Technological Change*			*Technological Change*		
	Relatively Higher	*Similar*	*Relatively Lower*	*Relatively Higher*	*Similar*	*Relatively Lower*	*Relatively Higher*	*Similar*	*Relatively Lower*
Radically new	1	2	3[a]	4	5	6	7[a]	8[a]	9[a]
Ongoing new	10	11	12[a]	13	14	15	16	17	18
Familiar	19	20	21[a]	22	23	24	25	26	27

[a]Not likely but conceivable in exceptional circumstances.

sure that an inbalance does not develop that will impair singly or in combination action range, opportunities, risk, or endurance. However, it is also useful for firms in lower-technology industries. They may, for instance, be able to build sufficient competence to upgrade the level of technology sophistication and thus gain a larger market share before other companies can catch up.

The second combilevel example brings together three key relationships that were used in the typification of the example firm in chapter 5, though in a different context. Inflation impact on the profitability of projects is a combilevel that relates the inflation sensitivity of projects' revenue (glossary item 29) and costs (item 28) to the degree of inflation in geographic areas (item 27). These characterization factors, when quantified as tracking levels, form the survey shown in table 9-2.

The distribution of invested capital for each SBU can be broken down by geographic areas and, depending on the relationship between the inflation sensitivity of revenues and costs, can be allocated to a particular cell of the table. When all SBUs have been treated in this way, the preliminary entry in each cell represents the sum of the capital requirements (the weights) for SBUs falling within that cell. As these data are then divided by the total capital requirements of all current projects, the resulting entry in each cell is the percentage of total current projects for that cell. As an alternative specification that may be appropriate for some applications, the net cash flow from projects in the geographic areas can be used as weights instead of capital requirements. In this case, the divisor is the aggregate net cash flow for the whole firm under study.

In addition to each cell by itself, the percentage aggregated from the following groups of numbered cells can be particularly important as steering ratios for managing the project set:

Projects with greater cost than revenue sensitivity	= 4 + 7 + 8 + 13 + 16 + 17 + 22 + 25 + 26.
Projects with greater revenue than cost sensitivity	= 2 + 3 + 6 + 11 + 12 + 15 + 20 + 21 + 24.
Projects in which the firm is particularly vulnerable to inflation	= 4 + 7 + 8.
Projects in which the firm is particularly benefited by inflation	= 2 + 3 + 6.

By prospective tracking of the various steering indicators, the company is in a

Table 9-2. Projects' Inflation Impact Indication

Degree of Inflation in Geographic Areas	*Inflation Sensitivity of Revenues*								
	Relatively Higher			*Similar*			*Relatively Lower*		
	Inflation Sensitivity of Cost			*Inflation Sensitivity of Cost*			*Inflation Sensitivity of Cost*		
	Relatively Higher	*Similar*	*Relatively Lower*	*Relatively Higher*	*Similar*	*Relatively Lower*	*Relatively Higher*	*Similar*	*Relatively Lower*
Relatively higher	1	2	3	4	5	6	7	8	9
Similar	10	11	12	13	14	15	16	17	18
Relatively lower	19	20	21	22	23	24	25	26	27

much better position to gauge the possible consequences of worldwide inflation on its operations. With this information, coordinated production schedules, financing arrangements, and even capital investment schedules can be articulated to minimize the ill effects of inflation and, sometimes, to capitalize on inflation-created opportunities. This is particularly true if the weighting scheme is in terms of the net cash flow from projects.

The third example combines two characterization factors that were also used in the overall typification in chapter 5. Combining the concentration of cash flow by projects (glossary item 9) and the project-oriented concentration of sales (item 10) will yield the survey shown in table 9-3.[74] Unlike the previous two examples, the position of the firm in this case is uniquely determined by a classification scheme. It is also different in that tracking in the usual sense is somewhat inappropriate. That is, since the position is determined by a definitional scheme rather than as a proportion, any changes would be discontinuous jumps rather than slowly evolving changes. Thus, as a variant of tracking, after the firm is positioned on this table an arrow can be used in both dimensions to show the direction in which the summary indicator under study tends to move.

Entries in cells numbered 1, 5, and 9 (table 9-3) indicate similar behavior in the two dimensions under study. Cells 2, 3, and 6 are indicative of a situation in which the core activity is generating many sales but relatively little cash flow. This usually identifies a profitability problem with the core activity, particularly if the firm's project set is in cell 3. Entries in cells 4, 7, 8, 10, 11, and 12 betoken a situation in which the core activity is exceptionally profitable; it generates much of the net cash flow from relatively less sales. In the extreme cases—cells 7, 10, and 11—the profitability of the noncore activities is open to question and should be investigated further.

Individual tracking levels, families of levels, and combilevels are all useful to conduct an adequate prospective evaluation of the company's project set. The

Table 9-3. Core Activity's Project-oriented Concentration Both in Cash Flow and in Sales Perspective

Sales Concentration of the Core Activity	*Cash-Flow Concentration of the Core Activity*		
	Concentrated	*Dominant*	*Dispersed*
Concentrated	1	2	3
Dominant	4	5	6
Dispersed	7	8	9
Diffused	10	11	12

choice of levels to track depends on the specifics of the departure situation. Thus attention is now turned to implementation issues.

IMPLEMENTATION OF A PROSPECTIVE TRACKING ANALYSIS

Given the basic definitions and explanations of the various types of tracking levels that have been presented to this point, attention can now be turned to the subject of how to use them for following and reviewing the corporate project set. But before starting, it is important to keep two things in mind. First, tracking levels and combilevels are not the same as situational typification steps; rather they are devices to introduce more dynamics into the analysis. They show how the departure situation, with respect to the characteristics of the firm's project set that is under analysis, is changing between two points in time. Second, depending on the problem situation under consideration, a host of tracking levels and/or combilevels may be appropriate for the particular purpose at hand. Although rough guidelines can be given as to what levels are important for certain kinds of problems, it is imperative that managers exercise creativity in selecting those tracking levels that will provide the highest information content.

To begin a prospective tracking analysis, the characteristics included in the overall typification of the firm under review can be projected to the preplanning horizon under the assumption of doing-nothing-strategically-new.[75] This will result in a projected typification of the corporate horizon situation according to management's perception, taking into account such strategic status quo assumptions. In a manner similar to that by which a PARE position was obtained from the analysis of the company's departure situation, a projected PARE stance status-quo strategy can be assessed from the typified corporate situation. This stance, the *projection maintaining strategy,* will play an important role in tracking the continuing appropriateness of the firm's current strategy.

Management is presumed to have in mind a satisfactory PARE position from the point of view of capital market reaction. This was used in chapter 3 as the basis for establishing subgoals in the perspective of the four strategic elements, the attainment of which would, in management's judgment, result in a good reaction in the markets. Since change is not instantaneous but occurs over time, it is reasonable to define this satisfactory PARE position as that which management hopes to attain at the preplanning horizon. At present, attention is being directed toward the achievement of this position. This represents the *desired* PARE stance. Comparing the projection maintaining strategy with the desired PARE stance reveals the extent to which the goals of the firm can be met with the current strategy. If the two projections do not coincide, the manager can ascertain the size of the strategic gap that must be made up by deliberate action.[76] This *G*ap *A*ssessment by *P*rojected *P*ARE (GAPP analysis) is an aid for enhancing the implementation of the usual gap analysis. A financial statement generator or similar corporate simulation model, supplemented where required by other mainly qualitative judgments, can be particularly helpful for top management in applying this method. Many of the crucial interrelationships among variables are built into such a simulator and, as a result of techniques such as sensitivity analysis, among others, there is less chance of misspecification or oversight of important linkages. PIMS reports can assist in this connection in structuring experience and helping to make better projections of expected trends.[77]

After the strategic gap is identified by the GAPP analysis, attention can be turned to ways to find proper recommendations for bridging this gap. Relaxing the strategic assumption that is required to generate the projection maintaining strategy, suggestions for action resulting from the approach described in chapters 1–8 can be superimposed on the firm. With these altered conditions, the characteristics of the overall typification, applicable to the company under review, can be projected to the planning horizon. The *updated PARE projection* obtained from this modified horizon situation can then be compared to the desired PARE stance to determine the impact of the recommendations on the strategic gap. If a shortfall still remains—as it invariably tends to be in a complex and dynamic environment—fine tuning of the suggestions, based on the information from the GAPP analysis, can be done until management finds a reasonable compromise in this respect. As a useful follow-up, the revised set of strategic considerations can then be checked for balance by application of BIM. Once a strategy is identified that is satisfactorily balanced along the most important dimensions, management can focus on implementing the relevant suggestions.

Timely identification, evaluation, and reaction to "weak signals" is an important component of strategic management.[78] By its very nature, prospective tracking is helpful in this respect since great care is taken to provide strategically structured information that is also of central importance for determining the economic value of the firm. Early identification of developing threats and opportunities and reflection on appropriate actions to live effectively with the inherent dynamics is the essence of the PARE-based prospective analysis. However, in ascertaining and evaluating the consequences of weak signals as they pertain to possible threats and opportunities, analysts must be aware of the danger of overreacting to ghosts or spurious noise, thus aggravating problems of instability.

In a complex environment, the use of tracking levels and combilevels is particularly appropriate for projecting the strategic impact on the company of such phenomena as inflation or foreign currency changes. The impact of such events is spread out over time and is usually relatively insignificant in the short run. The long-term implication of these phenomena can be particularly pernicious if not checked in time by adequate strategic adjustments. These implications may be dramatized effectively through a prospective tracking approach.

The impact of task complexity and interrelatedness on the effectiveness of actions can be modeled in this way. These key considerations, so important in organizational design, are often neglected by conventional planning techniques.[79] By inserting the expected intertemporal reactions from these influences into the GAPP analysis by specification of proper characterization factors, their ramifications for the strategic posture of the firm are discernible and thus can be explicitly considered.

EPILOGUE

The preface to this book stated that our objective represents an effort to link the strategic management area to a theoretically sound and usable financial economic foundation. This goal was behind the development of all of the analytical devices incorporated into the methodology. There was also an important constraint that served to channel the direction taken: operational feasibility must take precedence over theoretical niceties so that the methodology can be implemented in practice. At the same time, though, theoretical validity cannot be compromised.

Potential And Resilience Evaluation by the four strategic elements—opportunities and action range together determining Potential, with risk and endurance defining Resilience—represents an appealing and sound foundation for effective preparation of strategic decisions. By anchoring PARE to an external benchmark that has been validated in the applicable capital market, directional guidance is achieved. The value of this guidance is enhanced substantially since it is possible to derive from the PARE concept a theoretically consistent satisficing approach to decision making in order to achieve the desired capital market reaction. Also, PARE focuses attention on issues at the heart of strategic management.

One of the strongest criticisms of most other planning techniques is that they are too narrowly defined and are not typologically grounded. They can lead to a misdirection of effort, to unjustified generalizations, and to a distortion of the strategic balance of the firm. To lessen the chance of this occurring with the PARE-based methodology, the Balancing Identification Method was included. Although BIM has utility apart from PARE, the combination of the two gives a synergistic increase in the ability to promote relevant, comprehensive, and well-balanced action plans.

These action plans are checked yet again when the dynamic implications are investigated through prospective tracking. The GAPP analysis is a powerful tool to explore at least the near-term intertemporal ramifications of strategy. Particularly when tracking levels and combilevels are employed, enhanced structural insight is possible that increases managers' ability to detect, monitor, and respond appropriately to weak signals.

The coherent set of methods presented in this book falls within the realm of corporate portfolio approaches, but clearly it differs significantly from the usual techniques in this category. Seven major differences make this methodology richer and give it greater analytical depth:

1. The analysis is based on a typological specification of the current position of the firm. By starting from this departure situation, there is less danger of unjustified generalizations and the resulting inappropriate—or even damaging—recommendations.
2. A benchmark or reference item, carefully defined to indicate an externally verified designation of "sound" performance, permits value judgments to be made about the direction of movement necessary to improve the competitive position of the firm under study. Such directional guidance increases the likelihood that situationally warranted suggestions will be forthcoming from the analysis.
3. The methodology is predicated upon and validated within a sound financial economic theory of the linkage between managerial actions and capital market reaction. Thus the analysis is able to demonstrate the various underlying interrelationships and indicate why the actions are appropriate, given the environment and the current position of the firm. From this come suggested actions to improve the strategic posture.
4. Multidimensional factors are systematized in an adequate classification scheme upon which the tool for management is constructed. This refers to the four strategic elements and two key factors of the PARE method. Many different considerations may be applicable to the problem at hand; their essence can be distilled into the two key determinants of the PARE position. In this way, many data can be systematically compressed without significant loss of important information.

5. Broadly based problems, either geographic or activity related or both, can be handled efficiently within this analytical framework. Also, more problem-specific situations can be ascertained and evaluated by a follow-up grounded upon the same methodical structure. Thus there is consistency of treatment.
6. The approach is quite flexible. The manager chooses the most appropriate variables depending on the problem situation under review. This greater flexibility than is permitted with most of the other methods tends to promote finding suitable suggestions for action.
7. Dynamics are explicitly recognized to exist; thus provisions are made to include their implications in a meaningful way. This is facilitated particularly by BIM and by prospective tracking.

This method—or any other device—is only as good as the input data of course. The PARE-based tool requires managers to define SBUs and geographic areas properly, real growth must be dealt with, and, just as important, managers must have sufficient vision and insight to choose and evaluate the proper characterization factors. When applied by able entrepreneurs in a conscientious way, however, the methodology in this book is theoretically and practically superior to the usual planning techniques and is operationally feasible to implement.

NOTES

1. General Electric Company introduced the concept of the strategic business unit, in terms of analytically meaningful segments, as the smallest self-contained business for which a stratgey can be defined.

2. *Business areas* are based on a subdivision of the environment of the firm under analysis into relatively independent regions that have their own distinctive trends, threats, and opportunities. For geographically diversified companies, they refer to distinctive geographically determined zones, taking into account differences in markets, as well as economic, political, and social climates. See in this respect, H. Igor Ansoff and James C. Leontiades, "Strategic Portfolio Management," *Journal of General Management* 4 (1976): 13–29, esp. p. 14.

Resource areas refer to homogeneous segments of the firm's environment associated with human, physical, and monetary input, each having its distinctive availability prospects. See, among others, ibid., p. 19, and Bernard Taylor, "Strategic Planning for Resources," *Long Range Planning* 8 (1974): 27–40.

Influence areas are concerned with the proliferation of a company's problems of social responsibility, constraints on profit-seeking behavior, and questions of social legitimacy. These areas refer to a firm's environmental segments obtained if the many sociopolitical influences are sorted into distinctive and different societal influence categories. See Ansoff and Leontiades, "Portfolio Management," p. 20.

3. See, for instance, George A. Steiner, *Top Management Planning,* Studies of the Modern Corporation," Columbia University, Graduate School of Business, vol. 8 (New York: Macmillan, 1969).

4. An example of how this can be done is given in Rex V. Brown, Andrew S. Kahr, and

Cameron Peterson, *Decision Analysis: An Overview,* Series in Quantitative Methods for Decision Making, vol. 11 (New York: Holt, Rinehart and Winston, 1974).

5. See, for instance, Alfred D. Chandler, Jr., *Strategy and Structure: Chapters in the History of the Industrial Enterprise* (Cambridge, The MIT Press, 1962).

6. For information on feedback-control processes, see, among others, Arthur E. Bryson, Jr., and Yu-Chi Ho, *Applied Optimal Control,* (Waltham, Mass.: Ginn, 1969), and W. Jack Duncan, *Essentials of Management,* (Hinsdale, Ill.: Dryden Press, 1975), esp. chap. 15.

7. See, for instance, Russell L. Ackoff, *Redesigning the Future: A Systems Approach to Societal Problems* (New York: Wiley, 1974); Frans G.J. Derkinderen and D. Jan Eppink, "Environmental Dynamics and Planning," European Institute for Advanced Studies in Management, working paper (1978); Peter F. Drucker, *The Age of Discontinuity* (London: Pan Books, 1971); J.W. Gotcher, A.P. van Gent, and F.G.J. Derkinderen, "The Influence of the Changing Environment on International Business Planning," Empirical Research Report 75-9, Nijenrode, Netherlands School of Business (1975); D. Keuning, D.J. Eppink, and K. de Jong, "Practice of Corporate Planning in the Netherlands: An Investigation in Twenty Companies," Research Memorandum 32, Free University, Amsterdam (1975); Herbert A. Simon, *Administrative Behavior,* 2d ed. (New York: Macmillan, 1957); and "Piercing Future Fog in the Executive Suite," *Business Week,* April 28, 1975.

8. See, for example, Duncan, *Essentials of Management,* esp. chaps. 2, 13.

9. See, for instance, C. West Churchman, *The Design of Inquiring Systems and Organization* (New York: Basic Books, 1971).

10. See, among others, H.I. Ansoff, D.J. Eppink, and H. Gomer, "Management of Strategic Surprise and Discontinuity: Problem of Managerial Decisiveness," European Institute for Advanced Studies in Management, Working Paper No. 75-29 (July 1975), and Alvin Toffler, *Future Shock* (New York: Bantam Books, 1971).

11. The term *killer variables* was introduced by C. Jackson Grayson, the former head of the U.S. President's Price Commission.

12. H. Igor Ansoff, Roger P. Declerck, and Robert L. Hayes, eds., *From Strategic Planning to Strategic Management* (London: Wiley, 1976).

13. H. Igor Ansoff, *Corporate Strategy* (New York: McGraw-Hill, 1965).

14. Frans G.J. Derkinderen, "Pre-Investment Planning," *Long Range Planning* 10 (February 1977): 2-8. See also Frans G.J. Derkinderen and Roy L. Crum, "Strategic Management of the Financial Resource Allocation Process" (Paper presented to the Eighth Annual Meeting of the Financial Management Association, Minneapolis, Minnesota, October 1978).

15. Frans G.J. Derkinderen, *Hoofdlijnen der Bedrijfsstrategie* [Highlights of methods for business strategy] (Amsterdam: Kosmos, 1965), and Frans G.J. Derkinderen, "Balancing Identification Method," Nijenrode Report 75-2, Netherlands School of Business (1975).

16. Frans G.J. Derkinderen and Roy L. Crum, "Situational Identification for Strategic Management: Preplanning Approach in Diverse Perspectives" (Paper presented to the Seminar on New Approaches, New Trends and New Targets for Strategic Management, Cergy, France, April 1978). See also Frans G.J. Derkinderen and Roy L. Crum, "*C*ardinal *O*rdering of *N*ear-*I*ntangible *C*haracteristics: The CONIC Method," Research Paper 78-3, Nijenrode, Netherlands School of Business (1978).

17. Chandler, *Strategy and Structure,* p. 13.

18. C. Roland Christensen, Kenneth R. Andrews, and Joseph L. Bower, *Business Policy, Text and Cases* 3d ed. (Homewood, Ill.: Richard D. Irwin, 1973), p. 107.

19. See, for instance, Eugene F. Brigham, *Financial Management: Theory and Practice,* 2d ed. (Hinsdale, Ill.: Dryden Press, 1979), chap. 12.

20. Ibid., Robert W. Johnson, *Financial Management,* 4th ed. (Boston: Allyn and Bacon, 1971); Robert M. Soldofsky and Garnet D. Olive, *Financial Management* (Cincinnati: South-Western Publishing, 1974).

21. See, for instance, H.M. Weingartner, *Mathematical Programming and the Analysis of Capital Budgeting Problems* (Englewood Cliffs, N.J.: Prentice-Hall, 1963); W.J. Baumol and R.D. Quandt, "Investment and Discount Rates Under Capital Rationing – A Programming Approach," *Economic Journal* 75 (June 1965): 317-329; W.T. Carleton, "An Analytical Model in Long-range Financial Planning," *Journal of Finance* 25, (May 1970): 291-306.

22. K. Larry Hastie, "One Businessman's View of Capital Budgeting," *Financial Management* 3, (Winter 1974): 36.

23. Such is presented in David Durand, "Cost of Debt and Equity Funds for Business: Trends and Problems of Measurement" (Paper presented to the Conference on Research on Business Finance, National Bureau of Economic Research, New York, New York, 1952), pp. 215–247; Franco Modigliani and Merton H. Miller, "Corporate Income Taxes and the Cost of Capital: A Correction," *The American Economic Review* 53 (June 1963): 433–443; and M.J. Gordon, "Optimal Investment and Financing Policy," *Journal of Finance,* 18 (May 1963): 264–272.

24. W. Ross Ashby, *An Introduction to Cybernetics* (London: Chapman and Hall Ltd., 1961).

25. For these dimensions of the business environment, see among others, Hastie, "One Businessman's View"; Gotcher, van Gent, and Derkinderen, "Influence of the Changing Environment"; and F.G.J. Derkinderen, *Strategische verkenningen van het investeringsbeleid* [Strategic identification of capital budgeting] (Leiden: Stenfert Kroese, 1976).

26. See, for instance, Sang M. Lee, *Goal Programming for Decision Analysis* (Philadelphia: Auerbach Publishers, 1972); S.M. Lee and A.J. Leno, "Capital Budgeting for Multiple Objectives," *Financial Management* 3 (Spring 1974): 58–66; and W.L. Sartoris and M.L. Spruill, "Goal Programming and Working Capital Management," *Financial Management* 3 (Spring 1974): 67–74.

27. In this respect, refer to, among others, Boston Consulting Group, "The Experience Curve – Reviewed V," *B.C.G. Perspectives,* no. 149 (1974); Boston Consulting Group, Why Costs Go Down For Ever," *B.C.G. Perspectives,* no. 152 (1974); and B.D. Hedley, "Strategy and the 'Business Portfolio,'" *Long Range Planning* 10 (February 1977): 9–15.

28. Charles A. Huebner, "Strategic Planning – Management Tool for All Seasons" (Paper presented to the Thirteenth International Conference of the Institute of Management Science, Athens, 1977).

29. Royal Dutch Shell Group, "The Directional Policy Matrix."

30. Ansoff and Leontiades, "Portfolio Management"; Robert Pethia and Maurice Saïas, "Meta Level Product Portfolio Analysis" (Paper presented to the Seminar on New Approaches, New Trends and New Targets for Strategic Management, Cergy, France, April 1978); Derek F. Channon, "Use and Abuse of Analytical Techniques for Strategic Decisions," Manchester Business School and Center for Business Research, Working Paper 37 (1977); and Frans G.J. Derkinderen and Roy L. Crum, "Necessary and Sufficient Complements to Strategic Planning Techniques," Nijenrode/University of Florida Research Paper 77-14 (1977).

31. S. Schoeffler, R. Buzzell, and D. Heany, "Impact of Strategic Planning on Profit Performance," *Harvard Business Review* 52 (March–April 1974): 137–145, and R. Buzzell, B. Gale, and R. Sultan, "Market Share – A Key to Profitability," *Harvard Business Review* 53 (January–February 1975): 97–106.

32. Ansoff and Leontiades, "Portfolio Management."

33. P. Lorange, "Divisional Planning: Setting Effective Direction," *Sloan Management Review* 17 (Fall 1975): 77–91.

34. Pethia and Saïas, "Meta Level Product Portfolio Analysis."

35. W.E. Fruhan, Jr., "Pyrrhic Victories in Fights for Market Share," *Harvard Business Review* 50 (September–October 1972): 100–107.

36. See n. 1.

37. F.G.J. Derkinderen, "Financially Oriented Categories of SBUs for Enhancing Strategic Analysis," Nijenrode Report 73-2, Netherlands School of Business (1972).

38. F.G.J. Derkinderen, "Meaningful Environmental Segments from a Financial-Geographic Perspective," Nijenrode Report 74-5, Netherlands School of Business (1974).

39. Derkinderen, "Financially Oriented Categories."

40. See, for instance Hedley, "Strategy."

41. Frans G.J. Derkinderen and Roy L. Crum, "Introductory Typification Methodology," Nijenrode/University of Florida Research Paper 78-1 (1978).

42. Ansoff, *Corporate Strategy.*

43. See Boston Consulting Group, "The Experience Curve"; Boston Consulting Group, "Why Costs Go Down"; and Hedley, "Strategy and the Business Portfolio."

44. Lorange, "Divisional Planning."

45. Pethia and Saïas, "Meta Level Product Portfolio Analysis."

46. F.G.J. Derkinderen, "Identification of Inflation Impact on Profitability," Nijenrode Report 75-1, Netherlands School of Business (1975).

47. Frans G.J. Derkinderen and Roy L. Crum, "Typological Surveying of Long-term Bankruptcy Chance," Nijenrode/University of Florida Research Report 78-2 (1978).

48. Frans G.J. Derkinderen and Roy L. Crum, "Scanning Approach to a Firm's Insolvency Chance Categorization (Short-term Risk)," Nijenrode/University of Florida Research Report 78-5 (1978).

49. Derkinderen and Crum, "Introductory Typification Methodology."

50. Derkinderen, *Hoofdlijnen.*

51. Ibid., chap. B1.

52. Ibid., chap. B2.

53. Ibid., chap. B2.

54. F.G.J. Derkinderen, "Synthesis of PARE- and BIM-Approaches to Capital Budgeting," Nijenrode Paper 76-6, Netherlands School of Business (1976).

55. Roy L. Crum and Frans G.J. Derkinderen, "Typification for Three Corporate Cases Associated with Resilience Problems," Nijenrode/University of Florida Research Paper 78-4 (1978).

56. Roy L. Crum and Frans G.J. Derkinderen, "Typological Suggestions with Respect to Resilience Issues, Nijenrode/University of Florida Research Paper 78-5 (1978).

57. Frans G.J. Derkinderen and Roy L. Crum, "Discriminating Power of Typologically Enhanced PARE/BIM Methodology," Nijenrode/University of Florida Research Paper 78-15 (1978).

58. Frans G.J. Derkinderen and Roy L. Crum, "Strategic Bias in Using Share/Growth Approaches without Typological Guidance," Nijenrode/University of Florida Research Paper 77-10 (1977).

59. Pethia and Saïas, "Meta Level Product Portfolio Analysis."

60. Lorange, "Divisional Planning."

61. Roy L. Crum and Frans G.J. Derkinderen, "Typological Illustration of Potential Problems by Using Three Cases," Nijenrode/University of Florida Research Paper 78-6 (1978).

62. Frans G.J. Derkinderen and Roy L. Crum, "Coherence and Distinction between the Strategic Elements Action Range and Endurance," Nijenrode/University of Florida Research Paper 77-12 (1977).

63. Adequate integration of the Potential and Resilience strategic factors is discussed in Frans G.J. Derkinderen and Roy L. Crum, "Product Portfolio Techniques and the PARE-based Typological Method," Nijenrode/University of Florida Research Paper 77-15 (1978). With respect to the Resilience side, Gordon Donaldson has devoted insightful attention to the problem of the resilience of companies. See in this respect, Gordon Donaldson, *Strategies for Financial Mobility,* (Boston: Division of Research, Graduate School of Business Administration, 1969).

64. Derkinderen and Crum, "Necessary and Sufficient Complements."

65. Frans G.J. Derkinderen and Roy L. Crum, "Monitoring and Typologically Identifying of Weak Signals by Using the PARE Method," Nijenrode/University of Florida Research Paper 77-20 (1977).

66. One of the favorable exceptions is dealt with by Ansoff and Leontiades in "Portfolio Management." Their approach, however, is not so typologically structured as the methodology in this book.

67. F.G.J. Derkinderen, "PARE and BIM in the Context of a Typological Approach to Project Set Preplannning," Nijenrode Working Paper 76-5, Netherlands School of Business (1976).

68. F.G.J. Derkinderen and A.J.C.M. van Hoof, "International Expansion of Business Activities: Typological Aid for Decision Preparation," Nijenrode Working Paper 78-7, Netherlands School of Business (1978).

69. Frans G.J. Derkinderen and Roy L. Crum, "International Expansion for Risk Reduction: Which Country?" (Paper presented to the European International Business Association Conference, Dortmund, West Germany, December 1978).

70. Derkinderen and van Hoof, "International Expansion."

71. F.G.J. Derkinderen and A.J.C.M. van Hoof, "Typological Approach to Country Selection Going Abroad for Boosting the Firm's Opportunities," Nijenrode Working Paper 78-10, Netherlands School of Business (1978).

72. Derkinderen and Crum, "Situational Identification."

73. Frans G.J. Derkinderen, "Prospective Tracking of Corporate R&D Strategies," European Institute of Advanced Management Studies Conference, Brussels, Belgium (1978).

74. F.G.J. Derkinderen, "Typological Methdology to Approach a Firm's Concentration of Cash Flow as Well as Its Sales Concentration," Nijenrode Working Paper 75-3, Netherlands School of Business (1975).

75. This uses one of the well-known concepts described in Ansoff, *Corporate Strategy.*

76. Ibid.

77. See Schoeffler, Buzzell, and Heany, "Impact of Strategic Planning" and Buzzell, Gale, and Sultan, "Market Share."

78. H. Igor Ansoff, "Managing Strategic Surprise by Response to Weak Signals," *California Management Review* 18 (Winter 1975): 21–33.

79. Pethia and Saïas focus on this omission; see "Meta Level Product Portfolio Analysis." In this respect, Cyert and March have to be mentioned as the first contributors to this important area. See, for instance, Richard M. Cyert and James G. March, *A Behavioral Theory of the Firm* (New York: Prentice-Hall, 1963). Joseph L. Bower, *Managing Resource Allocation Process* (Homewood, Ill.: Richard D. Irwin, 1972), is also important in this respect.

GLOSSARY OF CHARACTERIZATION FACTORS

1. *Accessibility for Cash-flow Anticipation by Project(s).* Refers to the extent to which management has confidence in its ability to forecast accurately the expected future cash flow(s) anticipated to come from the project(s) under analysis.

Reference Point: Management's perception of the accessibility for cash-flow anticipation of what they believe to be a normal or reasonably representative current project regarding the associated reliability from the business sector(s) in which the company and its reference firm are active.

Classification: Very reliable anticipatory; good anticipatory; reasonably anticipatory; poor anticipatory; very poor anticipatory.

2. *Accessibility for Cash-flow Anticipation (Geographically).* Refers to the degree to which management has confidence in its ability to forecast accurately the expected future cash flow(s) anticipated to originate from the project(s) in the geographic area under analysis.

Reference Point: Management's perception of the assessibility for cash-flow anticipation of what they believe to be a normal or reasonably representative current project in the geographic area under consideration regarding the associated reliability from the business sector(s) in analogous geographic areas in which the company or its reference firm is active.

Classification: Very reliable anticipatory; good anticipatory; reasonably anticipatory; poor anticipatory; very poor anticipatory.

3. *Availability of Specific Marketing Knowledge.* Refers to the extent to which management and staff of the firm possess information concerning the ability to compete successfully in the relevant market for the activity in question.

Reference Point: Management's perception of the available marketing knowledge of the relevant competitor pertinent to the activity under discussion.

Classification: Relatively higher; similar; relatively lower.

4. *Availability of Specific Marketing Skill.* Refers to the extent to which the firm has the ability, utilizing available personnel, to capitalize on its marketing knowledge relating to the activity under study. The distinction between knowledge and skill is subtle but quite important. Management might be incapable of ascertaining the important market characteristics upon which action should be based (lack of specific marketing knowledge), but once these characteristics are pointed out, management might have the requisite skill to capitalize on the knowledge. The reverse situation is also possible.

Reference Point: Management's perception of the available marketing skill of the relevant competitor pertinent to the activity under discussion.

Classification: Relatively higher; similar; relatively lower.

5. *Availability of Project Qualities Knowledge.* Refers to the assessment by management of the extent to which the firm posseses information on the project in question pertaining to how closely the product reflects the qualities required by customers and any needed changes to meet such requirements better.

Reference Point: Management's perception of the available product qualities knowledge of the relevant competitor regarding the activity under discussion.

Classification: Relatively higher; similar; relatively lower.

6. *Availability of Product-related Skill.* Refers to the extent to which the firm has the ability, utilizing available personnel, to make any product changes indicated by the product qualities knowledge concerning the activity in question. The firm may not deem it desirable to make the changes, but this is irrelevant. The distinction between knowledge and skill is subtle but quite important. Management might be incapable of ascertaining the qualities required by customers for a given product (lack of product qualities knowledge), but once these qualities are pointed out, management might have the requisite skill to make the necessary changes. The reverse situation is also possible. The product-related skill includes the firm's technological skill with respect to the project under study.

Reference Point: Management's perception of the available product-related skill of the relevant competitor pertinent to the activity under discussion.

Classification: Relatively higher; similar; relatively lower.

7. *Cash-flow Margin of the Firm.* Refers to the amount of net cash flow generated for each dollar of sales.

Reference Point: The value of this ratio for the reference firm.

Classification: Relatively higher; similar; relatively lower.

It is possible to define this factor in relative terms based upon the reference point and in absolute terms. Since quantitative data are available to use in the calculation of this ratio for both the firm in question and the reference firm, the relative classification "similar" will be used when the ratio of the firm is within ±10 percent of the ratio of the reference firm. Otherwise the appropriate extreme classification will be valid. The absolute measure of the cash-flow margin of the firm should not be ignored in the project set management process since it has an important information content apart from and in addition to the relative measure.

8. *Cash-flow Transferability of Generated Profits.* From the firm's projects within a geographic area under study, this refers to the extent to which host governments place restrictions on the movement of generated profits to other elements of the firm outside the host country.

Reference Point: The median country of all countries in which the company or its reference firm are active arrayed according to management's perception of the transferability of generated projects.

Classification: Extremely high; relatively higher; similar; relatively lower; zero.

9. *Concentration of Cash Flow by Project(s).* Refers primarily to the relative financial importance of the firm's core activity or the extent to which the total net cash flow of the firm is generated by the core activity.

Reference Point: None. The classification scheme determines, by strict definition of terms, which category will be valid.

Classification: Core cash flow concentrated; core cash flow dominant; core cash flow dispersed.

Core cash flow concentrated means that the net cash-flow expectation for the core activity, A_c^f, is higher than the net cash-flow expectation for the aggregation of the noncore activities, $A_{\not{c}}^f$.

Core cash flow dominant means that the net cash-flow expectation for the core activity, A_c^f, is less than for the aggregated noncore activities, $A_{\not{c}}^f$, but is substantially higher than for any separate noncore activity.

Core cash flow dispersed means that the net cash-flow expectation for the core activity, A_c^f, is low, but higher than that of any separate noncore activity.

10. *Concentration of Sales by Project(s).* Refers to the relative importance of the core activity in generating the sales of the firm, or the extent to which total sales is generated by the core SBU. (For the financially oriented definitions of the firm's core activity and the major activities subset, see chapter 4.)

Reference Point: None. The classification scheme determines, by strict definition of terms, which category will be valid.

Classification: Core sales concentrated; core sales dominant; core sales dispersed; core sales diffused.

Core sales concentrated means that the sales expectation for the core activity, A_c^s, is higher than the sales expectation for the aggregation of the noncore activities, $A_{\not{c}}^s$.

Core sales dominant means that the sales expectation for the core activity, A_c^s, is less than for the aggregated noncore activities, $A_{\not{c}}^s$, but is substantially higher than that of any separate noncore activity.

Core sales dispersed means that the sales expectation for the core activity, A_c^s, is low, but higher than that of any separate noncore activity.

Core sales diffused means that the sales expectations for the core activity, A_c^s, is lower than that of a separate noncore activity.

11. *Debt Maturity Structure of the Firm.* Refers to the proportion of liabilities that are short term in maturity and that could lead to insolvency if funds are not available to pay them when due.

Reference Point: Management's perception of the debt structure of the reference firm.

Classification: Relatively higher; similar; relatively lower.

It is possible to define this factor in relative terms based upon the reference point and in absolute terms. Since quantitative data are often available to use in the calculation of this ratio for both the firm in question and the reference firm, the relative classification "similar" will be used when the ratio of the firm is within ±10 percent of the ratio of the reference firm. Otherwise the appropriate extreme classification will be valid. The absolute measure of debt maturity structure should not be ignored in the project set management process since it has an important information content apart from and in addition to the relative measure.

12. *Dividend Coverage of the Firm.* Refers to the firm's amount of after-tax income for each dollar of dividends expected by the market to be paid.

Reference Point: The dividend coverage for the reference firm calculated over the most recent five years.

Classification: Relatively higher; similar; relatively lower.

It is possible to define this factor in relative terms based upon the reference point and in absolute terms. Since quantitative data are available to use in the calculation of this ratio for both the firm in question and the reference firm, the relative classification "similar" will be used when the ratio of the firm is within ±10 percent of the ratio of the reference firm; otherwise the appropriate extreme classification is valid. The absolute measure of the dividend coverage should not be ignored in the project set management process since it is an important financial variable in assessing the endurance of the firm. Both the relative and the absolute measures of dividend coverage have high information content.

13. *Economic Circumstances (General) Geographically.* Refers to the assessment by management of the overall economic climate in the geographic areas under study. In this respect, the standard geographic breakdown in main and other areas for the project(s) under consideration deserves primary attention.

Reference Point: The economic climate in the median country, arrayed by management's perception of the attractiveness of general economic circumstances, from the point of view of the company's home base, of all countries in which the company or its reference firm are active.

Classification: Highly favorable; favorable; similar; unfavorable; very unfavorable.

14. *Economies (Learning Curve) of Project(s).* Refers to the relevant phenomenon of increasing productivity (at a decreasing rate) as new tasks are learned and experience is gained.

Reference Point: The assessment of the learning curve economies of the median industrial sector from an array of management's perception of the learning curve economies of all industrial sectors in which the company or its reference firm is active.

Classification: Relatively higher; similar; relatively lower.

15. *Economies of Scale of Project(s).* Refers to the relevant phenomenon whereby the total unit cost function of the project varies as the scale of the project is changed. Often there is a tendency to decreasing unit cost with increasing scale while the cost function is seen to be concave with a defined minimum at some level of production.

Reference Point: The assessment of the economies of scale of the median industrial sector from an array of management's perception of the economies of scale of all industrial sectors in which the company or its reference firm is active.

Classification: Relatively higher; similar; relatively lower.

16. *Environmental Change Regarding Project's Return.* Refers to the assessment by management of the impact of environmental change on the profitability of the project(s) under study. In this respect, the expected change in the project's return from the main geographic area of the core SBU or the main geographic areas of the noncore activities deserves special consideration.

Reference Point: There is no specific reference point for this relationship since it simply represents a relative categorization of characteristics according to management's perception of the impact of environmental change on the project's return on investment.

Classification: Substantial favorable change; small favorable change; no appreciable change; small unfavorable change; substantial unfavorable change.

When a single classification point is desired that is most representative of the aggregate of the main geographic areas of the noncore SBUs, the designation "mainly" will be appended to each of the classification categories.

17. *Fixed-charge Coverage.* Refers to the firm's amount of operating income before fixed charges for each dollar of fixed charges (such as interest, lease commitments, or redemptions).

Reference Point: The fixed-charge coverage for the reference firm.

Classification: Relatively higher; similar; relatively lower.

It is possible to define this factor in relative terms based upon the reference point and in absolute terms. Since quantitative data are available to use in the calculation of this ratio for both the firm in question and the reference firm, the relative classification "similar" will be used then the ratio of the firm is within ±10 percent of the ratio of the reference firm; otherwise the appropriate extreme classification is valid. The absolute measure of the fixed-charge coverage should not be ignored in the project set management process since it is an important financial variable in assessing the riskiness of the firm. Both the relative and the absolute measures of fixed charge coverage have high information content.

18. *Funding Capacity for Financing.* Refers to the ability of the firm to generate new incremental capital from all sources, both internal and external to the firm. To achieve comparability, it is stated as the total amount of new capital available for investment for each dollar of investment in current activities (book value).

Reference Point: Management's perception of the combined impression of the present and near future funding capacity for financing of the reference firm. Based upon industry insights and experience of the manager, tempered by external information and judgment about the factor from the firm's investment banker.

Classification: Relatively higher; similar; relatively lower.

19. *Generalized Knowledge and Skill Availability in the Firm.* Refers to general managerial, broad organizational and financial competence, and understanding within the firm under analysis.

Reference Point: Management's perception of the available generalized knowledge and skill in the reference firm.

Classification: Relatively higher; similar; relatively lower.

20. *Generalized Knowledge and Skill Requirements for the Firm.* Refers to top management's perception of the required general managerial capability, broad organizational and financial competence, and understanding for the firm as a whole.

Reference Point: Management's perception of the available generalized knowledge and skill in the reference firm.

Classification: Relatively higher; similar; relatively lower.

The reference point for this factor is the same as for item 19, generalized knowledge and skill availability in the firm, and is stated in terms of availability in the reference firm rather than the difficult-to-define requirements for that firm. Although this choice of reference point may seem strange at first, it has the advantage of introducing direct comparability between the availability and requirements side while still retaining an external benchmark.

21. *Growth Rate of Cash Flow by Projects(s).* Refers to the compound annual rate of increase in net cash flow available to the firm from the project(s) under study. In this respect, the core activity and the aggregation of the noncore activities deserve particular attention.

Reference Point: The median cash-flow growth rate from an array generated by management's perception of the cash-flow growth rate of all industrial sectors in which the company or its reference firm is active.

Classification: Relatively higher; similar; relatively lower; zero; negative.

22. *Growth Rate of Cash Flow (Geographically).* Refers to the annual compound rate of increase in net cash flow available to the firm from the intended geographic area for the project(s) under study.

Reference Point: The median cash-flow growth rate from an array generated by management's perception of the cash-flow growth rates for all industrial sectors in analogous geographic areas in which the company or the reference firm are active.

Classification: Relatively higher; similar; relatively lower; zero; negative.

23. *Growth Rate of the Market by Project(s).* Refers to the annual compound rate of increase in total demand for the products or services provided by the project(s) under study.

Reference Point: The median market growth rate from an array generated by management's perception of the market growth rate for all industrial sectors served by the company or its reference firm.

Classification: Relatively higher; similar; relatively lower; zero; negative.

24. *Growth Rate of the Market (Geographically).* Refers to the annual compound rate of increase in total demand for the products or services in the intended geographic area supplied by the project(s) under study.

Reference Point: The median market growth rate from an array generated by management's perception of the market growth rate for all industrial sectors in analogous geographic areas served by the company or its reference firm.

Classification: Relatively higher; similar; relatively lower; zero; negative.

25. *Growth Rate of Sales by Project(s).* Refers to the compound rate of annual increase in sales from the relevant project(s) realized by the firm. In this respect, the core activity and the aggregation of the noncore activities deserve special attention.

Reference Point: The median sales growth rate from an array generated by management's perception of the sales growth rates for all industrial sectors in which the company or its reference firm is active.

Classification: Relatively higher; similar; relatively lower; zero; negative.

26. *Growth Rate of Sales (Geographically).* Refers to the annual compound rate of increase in sales realized by the firm from the geographic area for the project(s) under study.

Reference Point: The median sales growth rate from an array generated by management's perception of the sales growth rates for all industrial sectors in analogous geographic areas in which the company or its reference firm is active.

Classification: Relatively higher; similar; relatively lower; zero; negative.

27. *Inflation Degree in Geographic Area(s).* Refers to the relative rate of increase in the appropriate overall price level indicator for the geographic area under analysis.

Reference Point: The overall degree of inflation in the reference country. The reference country is the median from an array of all countries in which the company or its reference firm is active, ranked by overall inflation rate expected in the near future, or, if projections are unavailable, by the overall inflation rate over the most recent year.

Classification: Relatively higher; similar; relatively lower.

Since quantitative data are available to use in the computation of this factor, the classification "similar" will be used when the inflation rate in the geographic area in question is within ±0.005 percent of the rate of inflation in the reference country. Otherwise the appropriate extreme classification will be employed. This factor is generally evaluated not in isolation but in combination with other factors. Also, it may be desirable to classify the reference point itself in terms of management's perception of what constitutes a normal long-run inflation rate. This may be particularly helpful if the firm is active in areas that all have either high or low rates of inflation.

28. *Inflation Sensitivity of Project's Business Cost.* Refers to management's assessment of the speed and relative magnitude of changes in business costs of the relevant project(s) in response to a change in the rate of inflation in the geographic area under study.

Reference Point: The inflation sensitivity of business costs of the median of all activities in analogous areas in which the company or its reference firm is active, ranked by management's perception of the inflation sensitivity of project's business costs.

Classification: Very sensitive; more sensitive; similar; less sensitive; not sensitive.

29. *Inflation Sensitivity of Project's Revenue.* Refers to the assessment by management of the speed and relative magnitude of changes in the revenue of the project(s) in question in response to a change in the rate of inflation in the geographic area under analysis.

Reference Point: The inflation sensitivity of the revenue of the median of all activities in analogous areas in which the company or its reference firm is active, ranked by management's perception of the inflation sensitivity of the project's revenue.

Classification: Very sensitive; more sensitive; similar; less sensitive; not sensitive.

30. *Investment Climate for Project(s) by Geographic Area.* A judgmental feature that converts into an ordinal ranking by management's evaluation of the attitude toward business in general and the specific project in particular in the geographic area under consideration.

Reference Point: The assessment of the attractiveness of the investment climate in the median country of all countries in which the company or its reference firm is active, arrayed with respect to management's perception of the investment climate from the point of view of the company's home base.

Classification: Highly attractive; more attractive; similarly attractive; less attractive; unattractive.

31. *Leverage (Operating) of the Firm.* Measures the impact of a change in sales on earnings before interest and tax of the firm and is the percentage change in earnings before interest and tax associated with a 1 percent change in sales.

Reference Point: Management's perception of the degree of operating leverage associated with the current activities of the reference firm.

Classification: Relatively higher; similar; relatively lower.

It is possible to define this factor in relative terms based upon the reference point and in absolute terms. The absolute measure of the operating leverage of the firm should not be ignored in the project set management process since it has important information content apart from and in addition to the relative measure.

32. *Leverage (Operating) by Project(s).* Measures the impact of a change in sales on earnings before interest and tax and is the percentage change in earnings before interest and tax associated with a 1 percent change in sales for the project(s) under study.

Reference Point: Management's perception of the degree of operating leverage for the relevant competitor in the activity(ies) under discussion.

Classification: Relatively higher; similar; relatively lower.

33. *Leverage (Total) of the Firm.* Measures the impact of a change in sales on taxable income of the firm and is the percentage change in taxable income associated with a 1 percent change in sales.

Reference Point: Management's perception of the degree of total leverage associated with the current activities of the reference firm.

Classification: Relatively higher; similar; relatively lower.

It is possible to define this factor in relative terms based upon the reference point and in absolute terms. The absolute measure of the total leverage of the firm should not be ignored in the project set management process since it has important information content apart from and in addition to the relative measure.

34. *Liquidity (Short-term).* Refers to the dollar amount of cash plus unused short-term borrowing capacity (lines of credit) of the firm per dollar of current liabilities.

Reference Point: Management's perception of the amount of short-term liquidity possessed by the reference firm.

Classification: Relatively higher; similar; relatively lower.

It is possible to define this factor in relative terms based upon the reference point and in absolute terms. Quantitative estimates of short-term liquidity for the own firm should be available with sufficient accuracy to be used in an absolute sense. Neither the absolute nor the relative measure should be ignored in the project set management process.

35. *Market Share (Comparative) by Project(s).* Refers to the percentage of total market demand for the relevant activity held by the firm relative to the market share of the relevant competitor. In this respect, the core activity and the aggregation of noncore activities deserve particular attention.

Reference Point: Management's perception of the share held by the relevant competitor in the market under discussion.

Classification: Relatively higher; similar; relatively lower.

36. *Market Familiarity.* Refers to the extent to which management has confidence in its experience and ability to compete in the market relevant to the project(s) in question. In reflecting on marketing familiarity, it is important to consider the extent and nature of environmental uncertainties in the market in conjunction with the assessment of the firm's experience and ability to deal effectively and efficiently with the relevant market possibilities.

Reference Point: None. The classification scheme is built upon an assessment by management of the category that best describes the market familiarity of the firm for the project(s) in question.

Classification: Familiar; ongoing new (with few unique elements); radically new.

37. *Planned-to-Current Projects.* The number of dollars that will be devoted by the firm to planned projects per dollar of current projects.

Reference Point: Management's perception of the firm's level of planned to current projects for a normal period.

Classification: Relatively higher; similar; relatively lower.

This factor has an internal benchmark because it is generally unrealistic to believe that management can have reliable knowledge about the future investment plans of other firms, such as the reference firm. (If, however, management does possess this knowledge, then the external reference point is preferred.) If the situation requires, the definition of current projects (see chapter 4) can be modified to include only projects currently being exploited. Planned projects would then include all projects not being currently exploited—both with and without commitments—and perhaps even including anticipated possibilities.

38. *Product Price (Relative).* Refers to the relative categorization of the selling price of the relevant product (or service) into market segments referred to as high priced, low priced, and so forth.

Reference Point: The median from an array of prices of similar products by other companies with which the firm competes regarding the relevant activity.

Classification: Relatively higher; similar; relatively lower.

The category "similar" will be used when the price of the firm's product is within ±5 percent of the price of the reference product. Otherwise the appropriate extreme classification will be valid.

39. *Product Quality (Relative).* Refers to the assessment by mangement of the relative categorization of the quality of the relevant product or service into market segments referred to as high quality, low quality, and so forth.

Reference Point: The median from an array of similar products produced by other companies with which the firm competes (as regards the relevant activity), ranked by management's perception of the quality of such products.

Classification: Relatively higher; similar; relatively lower.

40. *Profitability Index (Operating) of the Firm.* Refers to the discounted cash-flow value of the net operating cash inflows from the firm's current activities, augmented, if required by the situation, by planned project(s) under study, the cash flow of which has been adjusted for the relevant economic interdependencies, divided by the discounted cash-flow value (same point in time) of the total capital expenditure involved. Thus, in terms of present value equivalent dollars, the operating profitability index of the firm shows the number of dollars of inflow for every dollar of capital expenditure.

Reference Point: Two reference points may deserve consideration for this factor. The first one is management's perception of the operating profitability index for the reference firm. The second is the operating profitability index for the project of its own firm perceived by management to have normal profitability for companies similar to the firm in question.

Classification: Relatively higher; similar; relatively lower.

Although management would have difficulty estimating a numerical value for the operating profitability index of the reference firm, it is often not unreasonable to assume that knowledge and experience in the industry will permit management to render a relative ranking of the firm and the reference firm. If this cannot be done, an internal reference point must be used as a proxy for the reference firm. It is recommended that in addition to estimating the absolute measure of the operating profitability index for the firm's current activities, the measure also be calculated for the current set augmented by meaningful combinations of planned projects. This will reveal the intertemporal trend, an analysis of which has a high information content.

41. *Profitability Index (Operating) by Project(s).* An approximate after-tax but before-interest concept calculated as the present value of the project's net cash inflows (adjusted for any economic interdependencies with the firm's current activities) divided by the present value of the project's net cash outflows.

Reference Point: The operating profitability index of the firm's current activities (see chapter 4 for the definition).

Classification: Relatively higher; similar; relatively lower.

Since quantitative data are available to use in the calculation of this ratio, the classification "similar" will be used when the ratio for the project is within ±10 percent of the ratio of the overall firm.

42. *Profitability Index (Operating) by Project(s) Geographically.* Refers to the same concept explained under item 41, but it is also geographically applied.

Reference Point: The operating profitability index of the firm's current activities in analogous geographic areas.

Classification: Substantially higher; higher; similar; lower; substantially lower.

The classification "similar" is applicable when the ratio for the project(s) in the area in question is within ±10 percent of the reference ratio of the firm.

43. *Release of Net Cash Flow in Time.* Refers to the intertemporal cash generation or the cash requirement pattern of the net cash flows pertaining to the project(s) under analysis.

Reference Point: None. The classification scheme determines, by strict definition of terms, into which category the project will fall.

Classification: Primary short-term cash release with low long-term possibilities; high short-term cash release with good long-term possibilities; low short-term cash release with good long-term possibilities; low short-term cash requirements with primary long-term cash release; high short-term cash requirements with primary long-term cash release.

Primary short-term cash release with low long-term possibilities means that at least two-thirds of the present value of the net cash flow occurs during the next five years, and the net cash flows occurring past five years are below management's perception of the minimum annual cash flow required for the project to be above the cut-off rate notion. The project is a likely candidate for abandonment after the next five years.

High short-term cash release with good long-term possibilities means that the present value of the net cash flow for the next five years at least approaches the criterion for primary short-term cash release, but the net cash flows occurring past five years are above management's perception of the minimum annual cash flow required for the project to be above the cut-off rate notion. The project is expected to be a viable cash-flow generator even after the next five years.

Low short-term cash release with good long-term possibilities means that the present value of the net cash flow for the next five years is not a substantial contribution to the total present value of the project, but rather the net cash flow occurring past five years is above management's perception of the minimum annual cash flow required for the project to be above the cut-off rate notion and contributes the major part of the present value of the net cash flows.

Low short-term cash requirements with primary long-term cash release means that small annual increases in investment must be made in return for long-run gain. At least two-thirds of the present value of the net cash flows occurs after the next five years. These cash flows are above management's perception of the minimum annual cash flow required for the project to be above the cut-off rate notion.

High short-term requirements with primary long-term cash release means that substantial annual increases in investment must be made in return for long-run gain. At least two-thirds of the present value of the net cash flows occurs after the next five years. These cash flows are above management's perception of the minimum annual cash flow required for the project to be above the cut-off rate notion.

44. *Requirements for Specific Marketing Knowledge.* Refers to management's perception of the necessary information to enable the firm to compete successfully in the relevant market for the project under study.

Reference Point: Management's perception of the available marketing knowledge of the relevant competitor pertinent to the activity under discussion.

Classification: Relatively higher; similar; relatively lower.

The reference point is the same as for item 3, availability of specific marketing knowledge. This permits more meaningful combination of the two characterization factors regarding marketing knowledge.

45. *Requirements for Specific Marketing Skill.* Refers to management's perception of the necessary ability, utilizing the firm's personnel, to capitalize effectively on the available marketing knowledge concerning the project in question. The distinction between knowledge and skill is subtle but quite important. Management might be incapable of ascertaining the important market characteristics upon which action should be based (lack of specific marketing knowledge), but once these characteristics are pointed out, management might have the requisite skill to capitalize on the knowledge. The reverse situation is also possible.

Reference Point: Management's perception of the available marketing skill of the relevant competitor pertinent to the activity under discussion.

Classification: Relatively higher; similar; relatively lower.

In order to achieve meaningful combinations of the two marketing skill factors, this reference point is the same as for item 4, availability of specific marketing skill.

46. *Requirements for Product Qualities Knowledge.* Refers to management's perception of the minimum information requirements concerning how closely the product of the project(s) under study reflects the qualities wanted by customers and any needed changes to meet their relevant wishes better.

Reference Point: Management's perception of the available product qualities knowledge of the relevant competitor pertinent to the activity under discussion.

Classification: Relatively higher; similar; relatively lower.

The reference point for this factor is the same as for item 5, availability of product qualities knowledge. This permits greater comparability between the two product qualities knowledge factors when they are combined.

47. *Requirements for Product-Related Skill.* Refers to management's perception of the extent to which the firm must have the ability, in terms of organizational and technological expertise, to make any product changes indicated by the product qualities knowledge for the project(s) under study. The distinction between knowledge and skill is subtle but quite important. Management might be incapable of ascertaining the qualities required by people for a given product (lack of specific product-related knowledge), but once these qualities are pointed out, management might have the requisite skill to make the necessary changes. The reverse situation is also possible.

Reference Point: Management's perception of the available product-related skill of the relevant competitor pertinent to the activity under discussion.

Classification: Relatively higher; similar; relatively lower.

To promote comparability between the two product-related skill factors, this reference point is the same as for item 6, availability of product-related skill.

48. *Revenue Stance Regarding the Relevant Competitor.* Refers to the relative position of the firm's project under study in comparison with the relevant competitor concerning the ability to utilize learning curve economies, economies of scale, technology, and any other factor to enhance the net revenue of the project in question.

Reference Point: Management's perception of the revenue stance of the relevant competitor pertaining to the activity group under consideration.

Classification: Good; par; poor.

49. *Risk (Operating) of the Firm.* Refers to the unfavorable consequences of the uncertainty associated with engaging in the firm's business as measured by the relative variability of estimated earnings before interest and tax. This approach functions as an aid during the identification process. See chapter 4 for the ramifications of the firm's operating risk.

Reference Point: The coefficient of variation of the earnings before interest and tax of the reference firm, calculated over the most recent five years and adjusted, if deemed necessary, to reflect management's perception of the representativeness of the figure for the combined impression of the present and near-future value.

Classification: Relatively higher; similar; relatively lower.

It is possible to define this factor in relative terms based upon the reference point and in absolute terms. Since quantitative data are available to use in the calculation of this ratio for both the firm in question and the reference firm, the relative classification "similar" will be used when the ratio of the firm is within ±10 percent of the ratio of the reference firm. Otherwise the appropriate extreme classification will be used. The absolute measure of operating risk of the firm should not be ignored in the project set management process since it has information content apart from and in addition to the relative measure.

This factor should be checked for consistency with the level of operating risk implied by the interaction of the relative variability of sales and the relative degree of operating leverage. This is needed since the operating risk of the firm is a function of the interaction between these influences.

50. *Risk (Geographically) of the Project's Cash Flow.* Refers to the unfavorable consequences of the uncertainty that is associated with both project-specific and geographic-area-specific considerations and is defined as management's perception, for the project(s) under study, of the geographically oriented risk (political, economic, and sociological, for example) as far as it affects that project's business within the geographic area in question.

Reference Point: The risk of the relevant project(s) associated with the median of the geographic areas in which the company or its reference firm is active, arrayed by management's perception of the total (political, economical, sociological) risk of engaging in business activity in those geographic areas.

Classification: Very high; relatively higher; similar; relatively lower; very low.

51. *Risk (Operating) of Project(s).* Refers to management's perception of the unfavorable consequences of the uncertainty that is associated with the project(s) under study, taking interdependencies into account as far as they relate the project(s) under study to the firm's current activities. This approach is for identification purposes only. More attention is given to the ramifications of interdependencies in chapter 4.

Reference Point: Management's perception (estimate at present) of that activity of the firm associated with average or normal operating risk.

Classification: Very high; relatively higher; similar; relatively lower; very low.

52. *Risk (Operating) of Project(s) Geographically.* Refers to the same concept under item 51, but it is also considered in a geographic context; thus it is associated with the project(s) in the geographic area under analysis.

Reference Point: Management's perception of that activity of the firm in analogous geographic areas that is associated with average or normal operating risk.

Classification: Very high; relatively higher; similar; relatively lower; very low.

53. *Technology Change Indication by Projects.* As an indication for the likelihood of changes in technology, refers to the average annual research and development expense per sales dollar for the industrial sector pertaining to the project(s) under study.

Reference Point: The average annual research and development expense per sales dollar, calculated over the past five years, associated with that industrial sector perceived by management to have median or normal expenditures for research and development.

Classification: Relatively higher; similar; relatively lower.

54. *Technology Familiarity.* Refers to the extent to which management has confidence in its experience and ability to utilize the firm's expertise with respect to the technology required to be competitive in the market of the project(s) under study. The reflection of this leads to management's perception of the firm's experience with similar technologies and the ability to translate its technological capabilities into the relevant manufacturing processes.

Reference Point: None. Instead the classification scheme is built upon an assessment by management of the category that best describes the technology familiarity with respect to the project in question.

Classification: Familiar; ongoing new (with few unique elements); radically new.

55. *Technology Sophistication.* Refers to the relative distance from the state of the art of relevant technology development in conjunction with the degree of complexity in utilizing the technology. Both factors must be considered together since it is possible to have state-of-the-art technology with very low complexity (such as mousetraps) and very complex technology quite a distance from the state of the art (such as special-purpose integrated circuits). The interaction of the two factors determines the appropriate classification for the project(s) in question.

Reference Point: None. Instead the classification scheme is built upon an assessment by management of the category that best describes the technology sophistication of the project(s) under study.

Classification: Routine; average nonroutine; advanced.

56. *Variability of Cash Flow of the Firm.* Refers to the extent to which the net cash flow of the firm tends to fluctuate from year to year and is measured by the coefficient of variation of the total cash flow of the firm.

Reference Point: The coefficient of variation of the cash flow of the reference firm, calculated over the past five years and adjusted, if deemed necessary, to reflect management's perception of the representativeness of the figure for the combined impression of the present and near-future value.

Classification: Relatively higher; similar; relatively lower.

It is possible to define this factor in relative terms based upon the reference point and in absolute terms. Since quantitative data are available to use in the calculation of this factor for both the company in question and the reference firm, the relative classification "similar" will be used when the factor for the company is within ±10 percent of that for the reference firm. Otherwise the appropriate extreme classification will be used.

57. *Variability of Cash Flow of Project(s).* Refers to the extent to which the net cash flow of the project(s) in question tends to fluctuate from year to year and is measured by the coefficient of variation of the net cash flow of the project.

Reference Point: The coefficient of variation of the activity's monthly net cash flow, calculated over a four-year period one year removed from the present. The valid comparison is the relevant coefficient of variation of the monthly cash flow of the project(s) in question for the most recent year versus the same number computed from past data.

Classification: Very high; relatively higher; similar; relatively lower; very low.

The classification "similar" will be used when the calculated coefficient of variation is within ±10 percent of the reference point. Otherwise the appropriate extreme classification is valid.

58. *Variability of Cash Flow of Project(s) Geographically.* The cash flow variability (item 57) is associated with project(s) in the geographic area under review.

Reference Point: The coefficient of variation of the monthly net cash flow of the project(s) in the area in question, calculated according to the same procedure shown in item 57.

Classification: Very high; relatively higher; similar; relatively lower; very low.

59. *Variability of Sales of the Firm.* Refers to the extent to which the sales of the firm tend to fluctuate from year to year and is measured by the coefficient of variation of the total sales of the firm.

Reference Point: The coefficient of variation of the sales of the reference firm, calculated over the past five years and adjusted, if deemed necessary, to reflect management's perception of the representiveness of the figure for the combined impression of the present and near-future value.

Classification: Relatively higher; similar; relatively lower.

It is possible to define this factor in relative terms based upon the reference point and in absolute terms. Since quantitative data are available to use in the calculation of this factor for both the company in question and the reference firm, the relative classification "similar" will be used when the factor for the company is within ±10 percent of the factor for the reference firm. Otherwise the appropriate extreme classification will be used.

BIBLIOGRAPHY

Ackoff, Russell L. *Redesigning the Future: A Systems Approach to Societal Problems.* New York: John Wiley and Sons, 1974.

Ansoff, H. Igor. *Corporate Strategy.* New York: McGraw-Hill, 1965.

——. "Managing Strategic Surprise by Response to Weak Signals." *California Management Review* 18 (Winter 1975): 27–33.

Ansoff, H. Igor; Roger P. Declerck; and Robert L. Hays, eds. *From Strategic Planning to Strategic Management.* London: John Wiley and Sons, 1976.

Ansoff, H.I.; D.J. Eppink; and H. Gomer. "Management of Strategic Surprise and Discontinuity: Problem of Managerial Decisiveness." European Institute Advanced Studies in Management, Working Paper No. 75-29, July 1975.

Ansoff, H. Igor, and James C. Leontiades. "Strategic Portfolio Management." *Journal of General Management* 4, (January 1976): 13–29.

Ashby, W. Ross. *An Introduction to Cybernetics.* London: Chapman and Hall, Ltd., 1961.

Baumol, W.J., and R.D. Quandt. "Investment and Discount Rates under Capital Rationing – A Programming Approach." *Economic Journal* 75 (June 1965): 317–329.

Boston Consulting Group. "The Experience Curve – Reviewed V." *BCG Perspectives,* no. 149 (1974).

——. "Why Costs Go Down For Ever." *BCG Perspectives,* no. 152 (1974).

Bower, Joseph L. *Managing the Resource Allocation Process.* Homewood, Ill.: Richard D. Irwin, 1972.

Brigham, Eugene F. *Financial Management: Theory and Practice.* 2d ed. Hinsdale, Ill.: Dryden Press, 1979.

Brown, Rex V.; Andrew S. Kahr; and Cameron Peterson. *Decision Analysis: An Overview.* Series in Quantitative Methods for Decision Making, Vol. II. New York: Holt, Rinehart and Winston, 1974.

Bryson, Jr., Arthur E., and Yu-Chi Ho. *Applied Optimal Control.* Waltham, Mass.: Ginn and Company, 1969.

Buzzell, R.; B. Gale; and R. Sultan. "Market Share – A Key to Profitability." *Harvard Business Review* 53 (January–February 1975): 97–106.

Carleton, W.T. "An Analytical Model in Long-Range Financial Planning." *Journal of Finance* 25, (May 1970): 291–301.

Chandler, Jr., Alfred D. *Strategy and Structure: Chapters in the History of the Industrial Enterprise.* Cambridge, Mass.: M.I.T. Press, 1962.

Channon, Derek F. "Use and Abuse of Analytical Techniques for Strategic Decisions." Manchester Business School and Center for Business Research, Working Paper 37, 1977.

Christensen, C. Roland; Kenneth R. Andrews; and Joseph L. Bower. *Business Policy, Text and Cases.* 3d ed. Homewood, Ill.: Richard D. Irwin, 1973.

Churchman, C. West. *Challenge to Reason.* New York: McGraw-Hill, 1968.

——. *The Design of Inquiring Systems: Basic Concepts of Systems and Organization.* New York: Basic Books, 1971.

Crum, Roy L., and Frans G.J. Derkinderen. "Typification for Three Corporate Cases Associated with Resilience Problems." Nijenrode/University of Florida Research Paper 78-4, 1978.

——. "Typological Suggestions with Respect to Resilience Issues." Nijenrode/University of Florida Research Paper 78-5, 1978.

——. "Typological Illustrations of Potential Problems by Using Three Cases." Nijenrode/University of Florida Research Paper 78-6, 1978.

Cyert, Richard M., and James G. March. *A Behavioral Theory of the Firm.* Englewood Cliffs, N.J.: Prentice-Hall, 1963.

Derkinderen, F.G.J. *Hoofdlijnen der Bedrijfstrategie* [Highlights of methods for business strategy]. Amsterdam: Kosmos, 1965.

——. *Strategische verkenningen van het Investeringsbeleid* [Strategic identification of capital budgeting]. Leiden, Netherlands: Stenfert Kroese, 1976.

——. "Prospective Tracking of Corporate R&D Strategies." Paper presented at the European Institute of Advanced Management Studies Conference, Brussels, Belgium, 1978.

——. "Pre-Investment Planning." *Long Range Planning* 10 (February 1977): 2–8.

——. "Financially-oriented Categories of SBUs for Enhancing Strategic Analysis." Nijenrode Report 73-2, Netherlands School of Business, 1973.

——. "Meaningful Environment Segments from a Financial-Geographic Perspective." Nijenrode Report 74-5, Netherlands School of Business, 1974.

——. "Identification of Inflation Impact on Profitability." Nijenrode Report 75-1, Netherlands School of Business, 1975.

——. "Balancing Identification Method." Nijenrode Report 75-2, Netherlands School of Business, 1975.

——. "Typological Methodology to Approach a Firm's Concentration of Cashflow as Well as Its Sales Concentration." Nijenrode Working Paper 75-3, Netherlands School of Business, 1975.

——. "PARE and BIM in the Context of a Typological Approach to Project Set Preplanning." Nijenrode Working Paper 76-5, Netherlands School of Business, 1976.

——. "Synthesis of PARE- and BIM-Approaches to Capital Budgeting." Nijenrode Working Paper 76-6, Netherlands School of Business, 1976.

Derkinderen, Frans G.J., and Roy L. Crum. "Situational Identification for Strategic Management: Preplanning Approach in Diverse Perspectives. Paper presented to the Seminar on New Approaches, New Trends and New Targets for Strategic Management, Cergy, France, April 1978.

——. "Strategic Management of the Financial Resource Allocation Process." Paper presented to the Eighth Annual Meeting of the Financial Management Association, Minneapolis, Minnesota, October 1978.

——. "International Expansion for Risk Reduction: Which Country?" Paper presented to the European International Business Association Conference, Dortmund, Germany, December 1978.

——. "Strategic Bias in Using Share/Growth Approaches without Typological Guidance." Nijenrode/University of Florida Research Paper 77-10, 1977.

——. "Coherence and Distinction between the Strategic Elements Action Range and Endurance." Nijenrode/University of Florida Research Paper 77-12, 1977.

——. "Necessary and Sufficient Complements to Strategic Planning Techniques." Nijenrode/University of Florida Research Paper 77-14, 1977.

——. "Product Portfolio Techniques and the PARE-Based Typological Method." Nijenrode/University of Florida Research Paper 77-15, 1977.

——. "Monitoring and Typologically Identifying of Weak Signals by Using the PARE-Method." Nijenrode/University of Florida Research Paper 77-26, 1977.

——. "Introductory Typification Methodology." Nijenrode/University of Florida Research Paper 78-1, 1978.

——. "Typological Surveying of Long-term Bankruptcy Chance." Nijenrode/University of Florida Research Report 78-2, 1978.

——. "Cardinal Ordering of Near-Intangible Characteristics: The CONIC Method." Nijenrode/University of Florida Research Report 78-3, 1978.

——. "Scanning Approach to a Firm's Insolvency Chance Categorization (Short-term Risk)." Nijenrode/University of Florida Research Report 78-5, 1978.

——. "Discriminating Power of Typologically Enhanced PARE/BIM Methodology." Nijenrode/University of Florida Research Paper 78-15, 1978.

Derkinderen, Frans G.J., and D. Jan Eppink. "Environmental Dynamics and Planning." Working Paper, European Institute for Advanced Studies in Management, Brussels, Belgium, 1978.

——. "International Expansion of Business Activities: Typological Aid for Decision Preparation." Nijenrode Working Paper 78-7, Netherlands School of Business, 1978.

——. "Typological Approach to Country Selection Going Abroad for Boosting the Firm's Opportunities." Nijenrode Working Paper 78-10, Netherlands School of Business, 1978.

Donaldson, Gordon. *Strategy for Financial Mobility.* Boston: Division of Research, Graduate School of Business Administration, 1969.

Drucker, Peter F. *The Age of Discontinuity.* London: Pan Books, 1971.

Duncan W. Jack. *Essentials of Management.* Hinsdale, Ill.: Dryden Press, 1975.

Durand, David. "Cost of Debt and Equity Funds for Business: Trends and Problems of Measurement." In *Conference on Research on Business Finance,* pp. 215-247. New York: National Bureau of Economic Research, 1952.

Fruhan, Jr., W.E. "Pyrrhic Victories in Fights for Market Share." *Harvard Business Review* 50, (September-October 1972): 100-107.

Gordon, M.J. "Optimal Investment and Financing Policy." *Journal of Finance* 18 (May 1963): 264-272.

Gotcher, J.W.; A.P. van Gent; and F.G.J. Derkinderen. "The Influence of the Changing Environment on International Business Planning." Empirical Research Report 75-9, Nijenrode, Netherlands School of Business, 1975.

Hastie, K. Larry. "One Businessman's View of Capital Budgeting." *Financial Management* 3 (Winter 1974): 36-44.

Hedley, B.D. "Strategy and the 'Business Portfolio.'" *Long Range Planning* 10, (February 1977): 9-15.

Huebner, Charles A. "Strategic Planning – Management Tool for All Seasons." Paper presented to the Thirteenth International Conference of the Institute of Management Science, Athens, Greece, 1977.

Johnson, Robert W. *Financial Management.* Boston: Allyn and Bacon, 1971.

Keuning, D.; D.J. Eppink; and K. de Jong. "Practice of Corporate Planning in the Netherlands: An Investigation in Twenty Companies." Research Memorandum 32, Free University, Amsterdam, 1975.

Lee, Sang M. *Goal Programming for Decision Analysis.* Philadelphia: Auerbach Publishers, 1972.

Lee, S.M., and A.J. Leno. "Capital Budgeting for Multiple Objectives." *Financial Management* 3, (Spring 1974): 58-66.

Lorange, P. "Divisional Planning: Setting Effective Direction." *Sloan Management Review* 17 (Fall 1975): 77-91.

Modigliani, Franco, and Merton H. Miller. "The Cost of Capital, Corporation Finance, and the Theory of Investment." *American Economic Review* 48 (June 1958): 261-297.

——. "Corporate Income Taxes and the Cost of Capital: A Correction." *American Economic Review* 53 (June 1963): 433-443.

Pethia, Robert, and Maurice Saias. "Meta Level Product Portfolio Analysis." Paper presented to the Seminar on New Approaches, New Trends and New Targets for Strategic Management, Cergy, France, April 1978.

"Piercing Future Fog in the Executive Suite." *Business Week,* April 28, 1975.

Royal Dutch Shell Group. "The Directional Policy Matrix".

Sartoris, W.L., and M.L. Spruill. "Goal Programming and Working Capital Management." *Financial Management* 3, (Spring 1974): 67–74.

Schoeffler, S.; R. Buzzell; and D. Heany. "Impact of Strategic Planning on Profit Performances." *Harvard Business Review* 52, (March–April 1974): 137–145.

Simon, Herbert. *Administrative Behavior.* 2d ed. New York: Macmillan, 1957.

Soldofsky, Robert M., and Garnet D. Olive. *Financial Management.* Cincinnati: South-Western Publishing Company, 1974.

Steiner, George A. *Top Management Planning.* Studies of the Modern Corporation, Columbia University Graduate School of Business, Vol. 8. New York: Macmillan, 1969.

Taylor, Bernard. "Strategic Planning for Resources." *Long Range Planning* 8 (1974): 27–40.

Toffler, Alvin. *Future Shock.* New York: Bantam Books, 1971.

Weingartner, H.M. *Mathematical Programming and the Analysis of Capital Budgeting Problems.* Englewood Cliffs, N.J.: Prentice-Hall, 1963.

INDEX